The War On Self

How I Fight Depression And Anxiety And How You Can Too

Daniel CJ Grant

DCJG Publishing Victoria, BC 2013

Published by DCJG Publishing

DCJG Publishing, 4052 Douglas Street, Suite 305, Victoria, British Columbia V8X 0A5, Canada

Cover design by visualarts

Published in Canada

ISBN 978-0-9919299-1-7

For my wife Karlee,
thank you for changing everything.

CONTENTS

Preface
9

Everything Is Black
15
Taking The Steps
19
The Health Part
25
The Reading Part
45
Be Aggressive
67
Be Better Today Than You Were Yesterday
97
Personal Greatness
125
The New Present
143

Acknowledgements
147
About The Author
151

PREFACE

I remember at the age seventeen sitting on the kitchen floor, in my dark blue hooded sweatshirt. The hood was pulled over my head and was large enough that it covered my eyes too. I sat there, alone with my back pressing against the cupboard, while the family watched television in the living room down the hall. At times I'd methodically walk around like The Undertaker (the WWE professional wrestler) during his slow entrance down the ramp and think about the present moment.

Personally, I've always noticed that depression sucks me into the present where I'm only conscious of 'right now' and anxiety revolves around a potentially fictitious future. Of course, anxiety can viciously attack with any present thought of what someone is thinking about you or how you think you look like to other people. It's an interesting game.

At that point in my life I was already a pretty good baseball player, but I was tall and skinnier then a broomstick. I hated that. I never wanted to be a super gigantic person, but I wanted to not be skinny. When I watched baseball on television, none of those guys were twigs; they looked good in their uniforms. I looked like I was wearing a jersey top two sizes to big, but my greatest fear was baseball pants. I wanted them to be long and baggy. This was before professional ball players wanted them that way. The only reason I wanted them loose was to hide my chicken legs, especially my non-existent calves. They hadn't created those yet, unfortunately.

Making a career out of baseball was a legitimate thought during my late teens, at minimum going out and getting a university degree because of it. The problem was that fear of being judged and criticized consumed me during those days and lingered for many, many years. It grinded my progress into a mental battle beyond my control. I loved baseball, but I hated the pressure to perform and listen to people critique me on how I played a game.

There were many periods when I just wanted to quit. Like the time I was eighteen and skipped out on a weekend baseball camp that was being run by a few college coaches from the States, because I was sure I didn't want to play anymore after that season. So I got drunk for the first time in my life with some buddies, had a horrible night trying to vomit so I could feel better, and went to the park the next night and had a solid performance. One of the coaches at the clinic stayed behind to watch me and within a month I was going to junior college. I started getting a lot of offers, but I didn't even know about divisions in college baseball so I went to the school that was going to give me the most money. I was lucky.

When the intensity of college ball started picking up and I evolved into a high level prospect for Division I baseball, the doubt and anxiety crept back in and there were once again plenty of moments when I just wanted to hang up my cleats. Friends I talked to about it couldn't understand. Our team was ranked number one the nation, a monumental achievement. I was one of the best players in junior college baseball and we were headed for the World Series. I was being given almost every top honor you can get in college baseball including 1st Team All-American. I eventually earned World Series M.V.P in 2002 when we won.

I remember during the semi-finals of the World Series a grounds keeper talking to me while I was taking ground balls to start the fifth inning. He was raking around my area to keep the dirt smooth and said, "You guys better win this thing, I have a lot of money riding on you." I laughed and gave the guy a reassuring, "No problem". I thought it was hilarious that people would bet money on a bunch of college kids, but at the same time I felt as though the pressure to win had been raised just a bit. I mean, I didn't want to let this guy I didn't know and who wasn't going to give me a share of his winning down. My head was way to messed up to just laugh it off completely.

On the final pitch to clinch the National Championship I was so filled with anxiety that on the sprint to the human celebratory victory pile I almost threw up and couldn't even jump. So I collapsed and was consequently buried at the bottom by thirty people. My focus turned to survival not victory - there's not a lot of oxygen available at the bottom of a human mountain, plus you are being kneed and stepped on.

As we were mingling around the infield waiting for the National Championship trophy to be presented I remember standing next to my teammate who I was sure would win the M.V.P trophy. When they announced my name it actually took a second to compute it. Did I really just hear my name? I had a really good World Series, but by my standards there was no chance they would name me the M.V.P. I remember thinking I was supposed to cry, but I never did.

A few of us partied hard that night and I didn't fall asleep until about 9am the next morning. The upcoming summer would prove to be one of the most interesting summers of my life. From gaining my first stalker to being stripped to my underwear by a couple strippers who proceeded to have a whipping contest with my belt on my ass, I also ran sports camps for kids. Every Monday morning about forty playground leaders, and the four of us sports leaders, would get together for a meeting. I think I threw up every Monday morning that whole summer and could hardly eat a thing until I got home at 5:30pm. It was a horrible experience coming up with excuses every day on why I wasn't eating lunch or taking advantage of free food. Just the thought of being around people who I feared were judging me with every move I made was exhausting. However, there was no reason for these feelings to hold any merit. They were all actually really nice people minus that one stalker.

My anxiety gradually got worse. The anxiety seemed to pop up without warning. Then over time it just progressively kept getting worse and branching off to almost every area of my life. The only time, at this point in my life, I was really comfortable was in baseball situations. Every time we had team meals I would eat as much as I could because I didn't know when the next meal I'd be able to down would come.

When I left towards the end of that summer and made my way to Cedar Falls, IA, I hoped the new start would bring new results. It didn't. It actually escalated the problems. I started having trouble talking on the phone, actually throwing up in a wastebasket while talking to people. It gets a little awkward trying to explain why you just disappeared for thirty seconds while you were in mid-sentence with somebody on the other line. I also started separating myself from other people, hiding in my room and watching professional wrestling and episodes of Different Strokes on television. *What'chu talkin' 'bout Willis?*

I was tired all the time and had zero interest in school. I earned a GPA of 3.3 at Parkland College but in my first year at Northern Iowa I did damage to my overall GPA which caused irreplaceable harm (even after getting a 3.3 my senior year I still ended up with a career 2.87, I think).

My issues were building and I wasn't doing anything to make them better. When I went home for Christmas break my junior year I remember we had a large family dinner at my aunt and uncle's home. Everybody from my dad's side of the family was there. I overloaded my plate with turkey, stuffing, mashed potatoes, and gravy, like I did every year. The only thing different was I couldn't eat a single piece of it. Each time the fork got close to my mouth anxiety overflowed and I gagged horribly. A strapping young athletic man such as myself should have been a dump truck when it came to eating so, of course, I was being bombarded by comments. I blamed it on my strict Chef Boyardee diet I stuck too in college and they seemed to believe me. *Just keep hiding from your problems, Dan.* That's all I kept wanting to do.

When I got back to Iowa at the beginning of January I understood completely that it was the most important season of my life. It was the year I was going to get drafted if I played well. I could get out of college and go play baseball professionally. I had worked hard to get to this point and the pressure to perform was on. But I was so tired and couldn't muster up any type of interest in any of my studies, plus I was anxious about everything.

Then one cold morning in January it happened. The day everything changed...

CHAPTER ONE

EVERYTHING IS BLACK

Everything is black. I have just woken up. I hear the sounds of cheering. The cheering stops and then starts again. I realize it's coming from my computer. For the last week I have been falling asleep to James Taylor's DVD, *Pull Over,* and if I don't wake up to turn it off during the night then I wake up to the cheering that plays on the DVD menu screen. Sometimes it's nice to wake up to cheering. On this morning, it was not.

I open my eyes and stare at the yellow pit stain colour that is my rooms ceiling. The whole apartment is this ugly yellow, in fact. Who knows, maybe the walls were once white and just aged to ugliness. I notice the black mark to the left of the ceiling light and reminisce about how it got there. It was from a baseball bat when I was practicing my batting stance. It happened during a night I drank a few tall glasses of Canadian Club Whiskey and ginger ale. Those nights were starting to become more frequent, but that was the only night I chose to play imaginary baseball in my room. Usually I would just zone out watching sports highlights or stare at homework on my computer which I would finish, but my grades reflected the effort I was putting into those assignments.

I didn't really hangout with my roommate too much. I liked to isolate myself. It allowed me far more time for self-indulgent thoughts to encapsulate and drive me into an even more depressive state. I was lonely - maybe by choice - and I was tired of school and baseball. My roommate and I didn't exactly get along anyways. Not because we didn't like each other, we just had different lifestyles.

As I looked away from the black mark I decided that lying there any longer would make me late for class. I tried to move my leg. It didn't move. That's odd, I thought. I then attempted to lift my left arm. It didn't move either. At this point, I was still curious as to why it seemed impossible to move. The panic didn't fully set in until I tried to lift my head up. I could feel my body desperate and fighting to budge but nothing would move. All of a sudden fear gripped me as if the grim reaper was standing to the side of my bed looking over me. What the hell is going on? The thought raced through my mind with veracious panic.

I didn't know what time it was. All I could decipher about time was that my annoying alarm clock had been buzzing and then faded. It always faded after ten minutes. So it must be 8:05am. That was the last I knew about time that morning. My eyes shot quickly around the ceiling and looked as far to my left as I could but could only make out a blurry computer and beams of sunlight creeping through the window to its right.

My mind was engulfed with fear, searching for any and all issues that would cause my body to turn into an immobile organism. I had just broken up with a long distance girlfriend - she made the call on that one - and my grade point average wasn't exactly the 3.3's I was achieving the year before. A week prior I had just gotten back from Christmas vacation and baseball was on its third practice back from the break. I didn't love baseball like I used to. There was something missing. My heart wasn't in it. It could have been the cold, or just being in Iowa itself, either way, I was living a very somber and emotionless life.

I urgently kept trying to even twitch but every attempt brought no success. All I could do was move my eyes. Then, fear placed its hand on my heart and for the only time in my life, I felt that I was experiencing my last moments of consciousness on this planet. With a slow pace I would compare to a very slow gas leak, my body began to lose its energy. I was scared and fighting as hard as I could to keep my eyes open. Methodically, whatever was overcoming me that day was winning. Energy dripped through my pours and my eyes became heavier with each breath.

The moment finally came where I believed that this would be the last time my eyes saw anything while I was alive - and they were looking at an ugly yellow ceiling with a drunken black mark on it. My eyes were moist with sadness as they closed, then closed some more, until I was back to a black world and they couldn't be reopened...

CHAPTER TWO

TAKING THE STEPS

...My eyes open and I'm still in the same position I was in hours ago when life felt like it was leaving me for good. I try to move my left leg. It moves. I then try my arms. They move too. I lift my head to check my alarm clock. It's 3:07pm. Baseball practice was scheduled for 3pm today. I catapult myself up to a sitting position and gaze around my room. I thought I would be more grateful that I would get to see this place again. I'm not. I'm exhausted and swing my legs to the side of the bed so I can slump over with my elbows on my knees and my head hanging low with no help from my weak neck.

I reach for my phone - one of those old fashion wireless landline phones, not a cellphone - and call my coach to leave a message. I tell him I'm very sick and hope that's a good enough explanation for now. I go online and search for the phone number for the university medical office. I call and book an appointment to see a doctor the next morning at 10:00am after one of my classes. The rest of the day consists of laying in my bed and watching sitcoms and sports highlights. Tonight would be the first night I haven't had a drink in months.

As morning arrives, I'm glad I can freely move and am genuinely looking forward to talking with a doctor. I walk over from class in my baseball jacket and a pair of team sweatpants - I used to be a fashion king you see. I tell the receptionist I'm there for my 10:00am appointment and she politely hands me a form and refers me to the row of empty chairs behind me. I fill out some basic information and hand it back. Ten minutes later I'm asked to follow her to a back room where I sit for another ten minutes. When the doctor arrives he looks at the form I filled out and asks me about my symptoms. After I explain my tiredness and what happened the previous morning he begins to ask me questions about suicide and harming myself.

I emphatically deny ever thinking anything like that. I feel offended by the questions even though I understand he is just doing his job. After I answer more questions about my physical wellbeing, like how my bowel movements have been, he orders me to another room where I'm told to sit on a table and wait for a nurse to come in. When the nurse does arrive she seems happy to give me a cup and tell me to go take a leak in it.

When I'm done she informs me the next step is rolling up my sleeves because she's about to stab me with a needle and take a little blood for testing. Here's the thing, I hate needles and I had never given blood before. To this day that has been the only time I have given blood. So I was nervous, almost pass out nervous. Once I survived that stressful incident I was handed a red lollypop and was shown back to the original room I met the doctor. He told me he would let me know the piss and blood results by next week and then suggested I take a walk down to see one of the schools psychiatrists. He was kind enough, as I was getting poked with a needle, to get me an immediate appointment. I was then labeled clinically depressed with a severe anxiety disorder. It was a proud moment. Not only was I as depressed as Eeyore (I used to get made fun of for my Eeyore-like reactions), I was as anxious as a mouse stuck in a corner by an attacking cat. The doctor feared I'd walk out of his room and jump off a building and required immediate psychological attention. I was given prescriptions for three different pills; one for my depression and two for my anxiety. This morning was not going the way I had hoped.

It was a cold, sunny day. The walk to my immediate appointment with the psychiatrist was nice. I enjoyed it. I found the building and took the stairs to the psychiatrists lobby. I had to fill out a form there too. It was awkward sitting in that lobby with three other students. I know what I was thinking. These kids must be in pretty rough shape or have some crazy mental issues to be coming here. Oh wait, I thought, I'm sitting here too.

I was escorted into a dim room with grey walls and a small wooden desk tucked tight into the corner. I was asked to sit in the chair next to the desk. I waited for a few minutes and was thankful I didn't have any classes until 1:00pm because this doctors trip kept expanding and who knew where I'd have to go next.

One thing I find hilarious and degrading is how psychiatrists talk to you. They talk slow and soft because it's supposed to keep you calm. I'd prefer if they talked to me like a sane human being and not someone they think is going to jump out the window behind them if they talk in a regular voice.

Before I knew it I was whining like a pre-teen who hates their parents for grounding them because they put a hockey puck through the kitchen window (it was a hell of a slap shot though I must say). It bothered me. I felt weak and helpless. Did I seriously have this lack of control over my life where I've now been instructed to take three kinds of pills and talk to this guy who doesn't even know me?

When I arrived to practice that day at 3:00pm my coach asked how I was feeling. I told him how tired I had been the last week and nothing could get me out of it. My proof was the Red Bull I was pounding while I was telling him this. A teammate nearby suggested maybe I had mono. I went with that.

The next morning I took my pills as instructed. The following four months would be an adventure in depression, hope, and lessons. I would tear my hamstring causing my potential career in baseball to vaporize in an instant causing my depression and drinking to take on even higher levels. The drinking problem peaked when one morning I showed up to practice still drunk, had the best batting practice since my injury, had my coach tell me to keep doing what I was doing if that's the way I could hit again, and then ventured off to Burger King with my teammates. I was just about to order a Whooper when soberness tried to enter the picture and I started to feel gross and sick. We went back to my apartment to pick up our gear because we were heading to Evansville, Indiana for weekend games. I passed out on my bed. I was woken up with urgent instructions that it was time to go. I didn't have anything packed so I threw anything I could find in my travel bag. I had to hope all my gear was already in my baseball bag.

We got to the bus, I sat down in my seat, and I passed out. Nine hours later I woke up just as the bus was pulling up to the hotel. It was right then I made the decision to get control and make changes in my life. I slowly took myself off of the pills I was taking. I stopped drinking so much - I know that sounds bad but there is really no reason to stop completely unless it's a true addiction. I have never drunken to the excess I did that night and never will ever again. I like waking up sober and feeling good far too much to over drink.

The results weren't instant but with discipline and tenacity I have overcome much of the anxiety and depression I was experiencing. It is something that only hits me when I'm struggling - but that's not really depression...that's struggling. I feel in today's world the word depression is overused and overmedicated. Sadness isn't depression and pills aren't the cure for a lot of people. They are doing more harm then good. I haven't taken a prescribed pill since that day I took myself off them completely. It's been the changes and the control to my life I'm about to share with you that has created the difference and the progress I am now achieving.

Life shouldn't be stressful. It should be fun. There are obvious stresses that will test us and overtake us from time to time, but the main purpose of our everyday actions and thoughts should be to have a blast and help people as much as we can. I took life too serious for a very long time; all the way up to my mid-to-late twenties. Since then I've been having an awesome time creating the best life I can for myself in learning about the wonders of the world and this crazy life we get to experience.

If you're ready to learn my basic strategies for conquering yourself, my thoughts on different aspects of the world, and helping the people who want help then I hope you enjoy this book. These are my thoughts so far. When you are reading this, some of them could have been changed. I'm always searching, studying, and reflecting on life and the world around us. Time could be infinite, but it's limited for us. Let's wonder together and live a crazy amazing life on this large piece of rock floating through space.

CHAPTER THREE

THE HEALTH PART

This is the hardest part of the book to write - I'm actually on the fourth writing. It was at the beginning of the book and was the first chapter I originally wrote, but it has been the chapter that has changed the most. The message of the book changed about three months ago. No longer was it a book with a strict message on how to live a better life. I think I can help people do that, but is it really my right to do so? Maybe it is, but at this point in my life I don't feel comfortable in doing so. Now, saying that, this book still does do that, but it's more about how I've done it for myself, and how it can hopefully help you. I've always believed that if someone starts a sentence with, "you ought to", or, "you should", it might be time to run the other way. You don't have to do anything. It's fine to suggest, but to tell someone that there is a certain way for it to be done is wrong. These are my suggestions. If they work for you then I will be the happiest person in the world. If they don't or they don't seem right for you, I thank you for reading and giving me an opportunity to help you make strides forward in your life.

The choice to shift the direction of my thoughts and words for this book created a viral blend of panic and confusion because thousands of words had to be deleted and newer, more personal words had to be written. It's been both challenging and gratifying. I think it's rare for a person's first book to be so open. I'm young – 31 as I write – and I haven't done anything controversial that makes people crave hearing about me as a man behind closed doors. Society is full of ego and self-doubt today, which makes it excruciatingly painful to open up and let yourself be criticized. The positive is that even if 7 billion people tell me my book sucks, I'll at minimum have a few people that will at least smile and nod nicely…potentially while slowly walking backwards out of the room.

I wanted this book to be professional looking and sound 'expert-ish'. I then realized there might not be anybody on this earth who has all the answers in any one subject, so I should just share mine and if they help one person then all the pain and torment of writing my words would be worth it.

As awkward as this chapter has started, I'm about to tell you my opinions on fitness and nutrition from a life perspective without any hoopla or grandiose promises. The 'how to lose 30 pounds in 12 weeks' or 'gain 3 inches on your arms' are marketing ploys that make a lot of money on a lot of lies. I'm going to take you through my complicated mind and tell you how the fitness industry is like a corrupt government and why you don't actually need all the food you think – along those lines anyways.

So without further ado, lets talk fitness the way it has never been talked about before.

What You Need To Understand First

The fitness industry is still incredibly young. For the last 50 years the fitness industry has explored and figured out what works and what does not. Now we (the people in the fitness industry) just cause trouble and test the waters to see how far we can push the limits until we get called out and thrown in the corner for a timeout. Crazy techniques have been 'invented' and everybody has the secret answer to six pack abs resulting in apparent unlimited begging from the opposite sex to rip your clothes off. What we are really doing is just yelling. Almost like the talking heads on television, the louder you are, the more money you're going to make. No matter what crap you are pushing.

It's a wonder how we haven't collapsed as an industry already - it's a joke. And the reason we are still viewed with some sense of professionalism is because most people just don't want to think for themselves. We lie to them, preaching they don't contain the proper amount of discipline to achieve their goal weight. Maybe that's true for some, but for most they just lack an ideal plan. Supplements are still relatively fresh to the industry and aren't going anywhere any time soon, but the supplement industry almost operates like politics. They falsify and create data that's not true to sell you on it like it's your holy grail to success. They don't really think about the long-term effects on their fellow human beings gulping it down. They simply think about profit – of course, there are some reputable companies out there, but they don't get seen as much as the big guns (kind of like politics again). It's amazing how ridiculous the whole process is.

We need four things for survival: food, water, shelter, and companionship. We need nothing else. My guess would be that over 90% of the world has never even entered a gym, yet they are no better or worse than us – are they? Think about that for a moment. There are over 7 billion people in this world. That means over 6.3 billion people have never lifted a barbell. As a western society we should be grateful we have this option to stay healthy. The fact that we can walk into a place and pick up loads of weight off the floor – and not be doing it for hours a day on a farm - is pretty awesome. Actually, doing it all day on a farm would be pretty awesome too. There are people in remote parts of the world living past their century marks and they just work in gardens, drink wine and socialize in the afternoons with friends, and then relax and read at night. They aren't looking for the latest exercise to change the state of fitness as we know it.

So why do we argue so much, and not just do it? Why do we feel the need to attack our insides with hazardous chemicals to help gain an inch on our biceps or lose an inch around our gut? Why don't we just live a healthy life, filled with happiness, kindness, and laughter? Why don't we love, exercise, and do whatever we feel is best for us without fearing judgment? Because that would make sense and the people who run the supplement companies and the people who are lying about their revolutionary lost ancient secret towards sexiness don't want to you know what good sense is. So they'll continue to find anyway to put their hands in your pockets.

Treat exercise as an amazing experience because it is. A pleasure that many don't know about or have never considered doing. Who really cares how many reps you do or how many times a week you lift? It's your body and if you pay attention, you'll learn what works and what doesn't for you. It's a journey and an experience. It's not a clear-cut solution.

Let's Make This Simple

I lifted heavy weights for years. I put myself, and have been put through, brutal workouts that crumbled me into dust and left me lying gasping for air. They might have helped at the time; I sure thought they were anyways. I mean there really isn't any proof as to how it will all help out long term. I developed quite a bit of muscle my sophomore year at college. I was in the gym for two hours, five days a week. I was doing everything the current industry tells me is a waste of time. Maybe it was. Maybe I could have gotten those results faster. All it would have done is given me more time to watch movies or play video games though, so in hindsight it was a good thing it took up so much of my time.

So let's be clear then that not everybody needs the fastest workout on the planet. Some like it; let them do their thing. Personally, I have phased into a body/nature approach to my health and it just works better for me. I will still do some kettle bell and weight workouts, but most of the activity I do now revolves around boxing, running up a hill, bodyweight stuff (ie. Pushups, pull ups, etc.), and just loving nature (hikes mainly). I'm not as muscular as I once was and I understand that my man status is taking a serious blow revealing all of this to you, but I feel great and suffer from far fewer aches and pains then when I was crushing weights on a daily basis.

Plenty of people have injured themselves from pushing

weights around (minor and serious) that it does put into question what they are doing. If little old ladies do too much loaded pressing a shoulder problem will eventually happen. It might be best for them to keep strong by moving around. If you're old and slip on the ice and break your hip – this happened to my late grandpa Grant – the reality that you perform dead lifts might not have made it avoidable. I'm not saying it couldn't have been avoided either. This is where the giant grey matter of personal opinion and beliefs come in. A few years ago I would have been appalled to hear somebody say that lifting weights might not have prevented somebody from slipping and breaking their hip.

So weights are bad? Of course not. They are tools to help us feel and move better. That's how we should be approaching them. I'm really starting to believe from watching the amount of abuse that bodybuilders put on their body – how much they eat and how much exercise they do – if our bodies are genetically meant to even attempt to be that size or look that way at all. For some reason we view them as the peak of physical health, but by the time they are in their speedos posing, their brain function isn't the best because of the lack of water and carbohydrates in their bodies. Now, this is not a knock against bodybuilders. The dedication and discipline to do what they do on a high level is incredible. I just don't think we should view it as such an incredible health standard.

As Carl Sagan, the famous American astronomer, once said, "we live on a pale blue dot." Why in the world do we take things so seriously? Have some fun. Stressing out about how much weight you are pulling is nuts. I know it used to drive me absolutely crazy. If I didn't lift as much weight as I 'should' have it ruined my day. It's insanity to let exercise control you, but many people have let it.

A New Anxiety

This past Christmas I talked with my cousin about fitness. I've always helped him with fitness advice, but this year, for the first time he seemed relieved after I spoke with him. In the past I told him what all the research was saying and what was working for my clients. Eat enough protein, do interval training, lift in a certain rep range. You know, all that crap.

I told him I was being truthful back then, but I was so caught up in the game of selling optimal fitness I couldn't see past all the unneeded shit. You could see his fear of fitness being sucked from his body. Relief took over. He actually said, "I'm so happy to hear this. It's such a stressful and confusing thing to be healthy these days. This actually gives me some hope that I can do this."

My first lesson on fitness: There are no styles of fitness, it either works or it doesn't. Find one that makes you happy and works for you. We should all be working on our health, if you're not you can't be fully happy. That's the truth, but overdoing it is madness. Counting how much protein you get everyday is demented. What else can the industry create worry about? At the rate they are going we are going to be worried about the strength of our stapedius muscle (it's the smallest muscle in our body and also in our ear).

It's kind of like every new super food that gets discovered. Out in the deep lands of lush forest and cool watered rivers there is a berry that holds powers to cure and forgive you from your years of processed food warfare. Making it better - and more affordable - is mass producing it into juice form with all-natural sugars. This once secret berry helped natives from this remote region live disease free and close to 100 years old. It is a miracle that for the first time it can be eaten in western civilization.

First of all, you don't need a secret berry. Second of all, if you stay away from most bad foods and just don't over consume them like a seagull picking through garbage willing to eat anything that stays down, you'll be fine. You might even live close to 100 years old. We need to start giving a big middle finger to the fitness industry, the marketers, and the people selling the crap they know better then to sell. Every time someone tries to sell you a magic supplement or a 12-week program give them a giant middle finger and tell them to shove it. It feels good; trust me.

How Strong Do You Really Need To Be?

I used to meltdown every time I saw a grown man barely able to push 30 pounds up towards the ceiling while lying on a bench. That was back when I would do 105 pound dumbbells for a shaky six reps. The industry has always, I think, gone through a macho phase where the big strong guys are caustic towards the average 'there to be healthy' guy. I was one of them. Still today I sometimes get that urge to just scream when I see men struggle to do 10 pushups.

Strength is important, and I'm not saying being weak is fine. Strength helps you stay injury free if you're smart about it. Overloading the barbell every week to test the limits of how strong you can be seems a little outrageous now. A couple years ago it was not, and through a constant battle with shoulder pain I could bench a decent amount of weight. I could also dead lift a pretty good amount of weight. My squat sucked, but I managed. My knee would hurt and my love for lifting dissipated. Talk to any seasoned lifter and they will have the same stories and the same aches and pains, which brings up a question: how strong do you really need to be?

Women are starting to lift more weights, which I think is great, but there are now women in the industry pushing heavy weights and potentially starting an aches and pain movement themselves. We get caught up in our own press and that's true for trainers as well. It was for me. I was the strength guy for many years. People would come to me to get strong and I did a good job at it. We did it the right way. I still love getting in the gym and lifting heavy, but I don't do it as much as I used to. I feel good too.

Of course I'm not saying that you shouldn't lift heavy. If you love it, then do it. Take the aches as they come and be smart about what your body can and can't do on given days. Today's strength is not critical compared to tomorrow's health. Our lives are a journey and so should our exercise program. Along with phases of life comes phases of exercise. Do not get caught up in the fitness hype that surrounds us every day. If you don't go to a gym, then you're being bombarded with supplement advertisements and ridiculous exercise commercials. If you go to a gym, then you're bombarded by anybody who wants to take another dime from your wallet.

The Shortest, Simplest Nutrition Section Ever

You know what to do. I know you do and you know you do. Processed foods? Limit them as much as possible. Vegetables and fruits? Eat them as much as possible – actually, get a juicer and drink as much as possible. Meat? Plenty of debate on this one, but if it doesn't make you feel like shit then it's probably alright for you but I wouldn't eat too much of it. I'd stick with eating more fish than any other meat. On a side note: All you dudes out there who feel the need to post that you're going out and eating dead animal flesh are idiots. You condemn vegans and vegetarians for not eating meat and then sound like savage morons gloating how you have ripped through flesh with your own teeth. We are proud of you, we really are. Another side note: I eat meat, so I'm not a vegan disgusted that people eat meat. Just eat what you want and hold back the urges to promote how cool you think you are to the world.

Drinking is pretty simple. Lots of water and if you want something else make sure it's some nice loose leaf tea or single origin coffee and drink them all black. If the tea or coffee is quality enough you shouldn't need cream or sugar. And limit your booze intake. It's a dangerous substance that can lead to fun, but also serious problems. It kills brain cells too, which if you're going after an amazing human experience should be considered. I'll drink red wine and whiskey - not together - if I want to relax. Rarely do I ever go out and get drunk. It's obviously a moderation substance so just use it wisely and don't be stupid.

I would stay away from bread and highly processed pastas. Spelt is a good flour to use or consume when eating pasta or bread. It's not very processed at all.

If you want to eat six times a day then be my guest, but I would seriously recommend just keeping it down to 1-3 meals a day. Eat the larger amount at night too. Eat smaller meals during the day and don't eat right away. Load your body with water and a fresh juice in the morning. Our bodies don't need a lot of food so stop feeding it like it's a garbage disposal.

Oh, and if my meal strategy doesn't work for you then don't do it. Be smart and find out what works for you. Education, my friends, should always come before motivation.

Education Before Motivation

Here is the unedited version of an article I wrote awhile back that was featured in the Feb/Mar 2013 edition of *Inside Fitness Magazine* that shows my point:

Why Motivation Is Dangerous

I deal with health and fitness, but not necessarily from a how-to standpoint. I don't tell people how to workout. I do tell people how to eat but all that usually boils down to are basic solutions if you choose to accept them and implement them. I talk a lot about our actions and mindset as a relation to the outcomes we get with our health. I mean, that's what it's all about, isn't it?

I used to be the fitness professional who stated on the top of my mythical pedestal that I believed that everybody should dead lift because it's the greatest exercise in the history of mankind. I used to dictate, until there was no tomorrow, about how if you didn't eat six meals a day then you were wasting both yours and my time because you were obviously not going to get the results. I believe (like a few fitness professionals) that learning your craft is the only way to evolve and actually help people the proper way when they hire you.

The interesting thing about it is that learning our crafts has all taken us on different evolutionary paths when it comes to our philosophy on health and fitness.

I still believe the dead lift is the greatest exercise but I now sure as hell understand that you don't need it to be successful. Six meals a day is 'hogwash' and in the case of my own experience is all a mindset to how we approach food. I used to be a guy who started getting the shakes and VERY irritated if I didn't eat every few hours. Now I incorporate intermittent fasting into my plan along with only eating 2-3 meals a day and I juice fruits and vegetables on a daily basis.

You see, I've never been a big fan of vegetables. Growing up they weren't around all the time and too be honest I'm not exactly too savvy in the kitchen with a knife (due to a childhood experience with a knife and one of my fingers) so cutting up vegetables wasn't on my priority list of things to do. So I generally decided to just avoid them, unless my fiancé was cooking them up. I knew, of course, I wasn't getting all the vitamins and minerals I should be and after noticing that my weight was slowly creeping up I decided that I needed a solution. Enter the juicer and enter my savior when it comes to health.

I've never felt so good and if for some reason I don't get to a meal or am busy it rarely phases me one bit. The shakes and irritability I once experienced was all due to my relationship towards food. It had nothing to do with my blood sugar levels at all.

I've evolved through my education in health, fitness, and life. I'm not as hardcore as I used to be when it came to what needs to be done. I still hate long cardio, ellipticals, the BOSU ball, most exercise machines, and CrossFit, but I won't start thinking less of you as a human being anymore if you do that type of exercise.

Motivation is Bunk

I've always wanted to write a book. I've tried many times to complete one; all attempts ended up in failure. I'd find periods of motivation and then I'd just write, blindly thinking that I was actually accomplishing something. Then after a few weeks the motivation would wear off and all I could see in front of me was a pile of words with no real strategy and no real prescribed outcome other then a physical product. I had no true vision of what I wanted or how to really get there.

I didn't take the time to learn about the process or even work on my actual writing skills (some might say they are still very suspect). I just went off motivation and my desire to write a book. Consequently, no book ever got finished. This year I took the time to learn how to plan and organize the writing of a book. I sat down, figured out what I wanted to teach, and then outlined how I would teach it. Low and behold, I'm already very close to finishing my first draft. All because I didn't bank on my motivation to write a book but because of the education I got out of researching and planning how to write my book.

I learned that same truth a while back with clients. They don't need motivation all the time. Trying to keep clients going with superficial motivation will only burn you out (it sure burned me out when I was a young trainer). They need education and they need to be smart enough to come up with their own thoughts and opinions. The best clients I've ever had are the one's that take time to research and not take what I say as an instant truth. From the first assessment on I tell them to not believe what I tell them and form their own opinions whether it will be good for them or not.

It keeps them focused and it educates them about their own health. I research a lot so I know I'm not making stuff up, but I want them to figure that out for themselves. My goal is to get them to treat their health like it's their craft...if that makes sense?

I mean, it's their body and their life and it's your body and your life. You should never take information blindly when it's dealing with YOUR life.

<u>Education BEFORE Motivation</u>

The issue I find is that people don't treat their health and fitness as a craft. They typically use motivation to get them going and once that motivation dies down then you can put the nails in the coffin because their journey is over – until the next wave of motivation comes their way that is.

This is why I think motivation is one of the most overrated aspects of life. Motivation does nothing but to get people all fired up and start taking action.

"But, that's a good thing Dan!"

NO IT'S NOT!

Listen to me, I'm all for people taking action and improving their lives but what if I motivated an idiot? **Then we'd all have a motivated idiot running around.**

I feel like this is what our industry has turned into. We can motivate the hell out of people by showing them inspirational videos and give them motivational speeches but if they don't know what they are doing then we have just that – a bunch of motivated people who have no idea what they are doing running around the gym.

You've seen it and I've seen it. They are the people who look like their backs are about to snap on every rep while they dead lift. They are the people who read celebrity magazines while sitting on a recumbent bike as they maintain their heart rate level in the 'fat-burning zone'. They are the people who think that absolutely murdering yourself every workout is actually a good thing for you. They shove ten different supplements down their throat believing that's whats necessary for a sexy body. They are all jacked up to get healthy but they have no clue as to what that actually entails.

I understand that's what a coach is for but many people can't afford one and there are many coaches out there who are not even properly educated themselves.

Education has to happen before motivation.

Your health is the most important thing you possess. If you didn't have your health then life probably wouldn't be awesome. So why not put down the trashy magazines, the mystery novels, and turn off the reality shows and start learning about the most important aspect of your life – your health.

Learn what's right for you. Learn the best way to eat for yourself. Learn what makes you feel good and gives you the results that you want.

Here's a bonus tip: Just because someone is famous doesn't mean they know what they are talking about. If they have a New York Times Bestseller, don't automatically believe everything they are talking about. Same goes if they train celebrities. You are not a celebrity so why would you try to do what they do…they have a few different priorities then you and most of the women are starting to look like skeletons anyways.

You have to try things out on your own. I've tried plenty of exercise routines from some of the biggest names in the industry. Some I loved, some I hated. Doesn't mean I think anything less of the professionals whose workouts I didn't like, they just weren't for me. Some people love my views on life and health, some think I'm too negative, some really dig how *I* tell things in a very real manner, and some don't hesitate to email me how I've somehow made personal attacks towards them (people I've never met in my life as a matter of fact).

It's your education and experimentation however, that gets you the long-term results that everybody needs. It's not through motivation.

So don't just search out motivation. Make the time to educate yourself and stop following advice blindly, that's what the mediocre do…and you don't want to be mediocre. If you did, you wouldn't be here reading this.

Learn A Discipline

An activity I currently love doing is boxing. Going to workouts is fun and makes me work hard. The main reason I love it so much is the heavy bag work, however. It's like meditation for me. It's just me and the bag.

Jab, jab, punch.
Jab, punch, hook.
Jab, jab, jab.

It allows me step away from my life outside and be totally focused in a skill. The heavy bag leaves me drenched in sweat and exhausted shoulders. It's an incredible feeling. I believe finding a skill has helped me stay focused on my fitness. Maybe it would for you too. Learning a discipline and dedicating yourself to mastering it allows the discipline process to blend over to your everyday life. You feel better and understand the work ethic needed to go after something important to you. I also believe that if everybody in this world studied and learned a discipline like boxing, jujitsu, or any fighting style it would make the world a calmer, happier place. I know that seems counterintuitive but I feel truth in that statement.

Discipline is a missing factor in many peoples lives when it comes to health and happiness. Learning a discipline can help change that.

Stay Focused, I'm Just Getting Started

Honestly, if you've made it this far you are either a family member or you are one of the few people who actually make it through the first couple chapters in a book. I urge you to stay focused. Not because I have anything groundbreaking to say, but because it took me a longtime filled with anxiety and questioning myself to write these words so you should support that fact. Just kidding.

The next chapters divulge what helped my mindset and kept me in tune with daily battles with anxiety and depression, which I now win 95% of the time if I'm going by the statistics I don't keep.

CHAPTER FOUR

THE READING PART

"The book you don't read won't help." - Jim Rohn

"Books are the quietest and most constant of friends; they are the most accessible and wisest of counselors, and the most patient of teachers." - Charles W. Eliot

"When I get a little money, I buy books. If any left, I buy food and clothes." - Erasmus

"The more you read, the more things you will know. The more that you learn, the more places you'll go." - Dr. Seuss

Impatience has always been a weakness of mine. Most people, I'm sure, struggle with it too, but I seem to have an unnerving distortion of true impatience. Needed, wanted, now, was an unofficial motto of mine. Information I couldn't gain instantly didn't process in my mind to be worth venturing after. So I didn't, and the result was an embarrassing list of completed books read that included The Great Gatsby, Bleachers by John Grisham, and Lord of the Flies. That was it until I was 27. To add to the insult of my efforts they were all books I was forced to read in school. Of course, books such as Lord of the Flies and To Kill a Mockingbird were mandatory but thank goodness they had a movie. Even books I wanted to read I couldn't. At the age of 12 I unwrapped Kelly Gruber's autobiography one eager Christmas morning and I was more than excited. He was my hero. He was the reason I turned into a third baseman and chose 17 as my all-time lucky number. I made it halfway through that book.

This was during a time when the Internet was not in many households. I didn't know what an email was, granted I was only 12. But if you're a 12 year old these days and you don't have a Facebook, Instagram, and a Twitter account then I'm sorry to inform you that you are way behind on the socially accepted norms in your young world. How sad did that make you reading that last sentence? It made me a little sad and worried writing it. The point is I didn't enjoy reading. I wasn't a dumb kid. I actually got really good grades when I gave it a solid effort, the latter part of that statement holding the most authority. Was my efforts depression related? Maybe.

Depression started bothering me during my mid-teenage years until my mid to late twenties. Why? I don't really know. I was a natural all-around athlete, grew up in a good home with great parents who provided myself and my brother and sister with anything we needed, and gained a lot of recognition as a promising baseball star. Honestly, you could argue that my life was too easy and maybe that was part of the issue.

After the depression inhabited me full-time for a few years, anxiety then decided to sneak its way in. Sure, there was a lot of performance pressure as far as baseball went, but from the social aspect of life everything hit me pretty hard one summer before I transferred to the University of Northern Iowa for the fall semester.

A deep part of me has always been afraid of rejection and failure, probably more than most people experience. My anxiety proved methodical and vicious, skyrocketing to incredibly high levels with me. It used to debilitate me so much that I couldn't talk on the phone without being crouched down beside a waste bin just in case I needed to vomit. I usually had to vomit. I couldn't eat in front of people and when I was alone and could eat my stomach almost rejected the food because my insides were so acidic from the lack of nutrients to balance it.

I felt out of control. I was out of control. Daily living was stressful. Not knowing how much food I would be able to eat that day made me insane. Then my promising baseball career took a sudden turn when my left hamstring exploded and the scouts vanished. I made decisions with money that were idiotic and built a massive amount of debt for no real reason at all. Along came sleepless nights and plenty of desperate thoughts. I felt life was treating me wrong. It was unfair and cruel to take away the opportunities I had worked so hard for.

My mind was lying to me. I was turning into a coward. I couldn't face my fears and all I could do was think about giving up. Maybe I should just get a regular, stable job. Maybe I should quit this little fairytale dream of being in baseball. Maybe there wasn't really enough time to achieve all of my goals and aspirations. My brain was telling me all of these things until it dawned on me that my mind needed to get stronger and tougher. Like physical exercise strengthened the body, I believed the same was true for the mind.

So I started reading, very slowly. Being impatient with the inability to not read and analyze every word is not a good combination. I had compiled a vast amount of unread books during my teenage and early twenties. I really did have good intentions and I have always loved books. I just didn't like completely reading them. I can assure you I looked smart as can be with my growing collection of books but with every purchase I was not getting smarter - funny how that works. You actually have to read the books to learn what's in them.

It wasn't easy for me at first. I would get frustrated. I would read and then reread to make sure I understood everything that was written. I would get impatient and upset that I wasn't becoming a speed-reader overnight. It was mental weakness at it's finest. Instead of just stopping, like I did in the past, I pushed myself to stick with it. I made a commitment to not touch another book until I had finished the one I was reading. As time progressed I started to get into the flow of adding reading into my everyday routine. If I had an extra busy day coming up I'd block off a few fifteen-minute periods to make sure I had no excuses. In fact, a book was always with me in case I found some downtime and could just pop it open for a few minutes.

Fiction vs. Non-Fiction

I must confess I was incredibly anti-fiction for most of my life. I just didn't find it interesting. I wanted to learn something. So when I did start adding reading to my daily activities it was all non-fiction. I wrote articles condemning people who wasted their time reading fake stories. Self-help teachers were saying the same thing to a certain extent. It was when I really focused my time on being a writer professionally that I became interested in writing fiction. The creative aspect of developing a story was fascinating to me. So I started reading some classic authors. Ernest Hemingway, John Steinbeck, and Mark Twain. I learned how they wrote and a small place in my heart opened up for good stories.

I started writing short stories myself. I wondered if you could be both a fiction and a non-fiction author. Steven Pressfield is a great example of that. Just like everything in life there is good and there is bad. There is good non-fiction and bad non-fiction; same story with fiction. Well-written stories and poetry can make you think and keep your mind sharp. This is actually hard to tell you since I was so opposed to fiction my whole life.

We can easily get stuck on what other people say. When someone you admire tells you that fiction is a waste of time you believe them. When it's a non-fiction writer who is telling you that, it is probably a situation where you need to put two and two together. Non-fiction, I believe, should still be the bulk of your reading. Now, I will mix in a classic novel or good fiction writing after I have read four or five non-fiction books.

I love to read books that really make me think. I read stories of great people, who triumphed against all odds and will be remembered and talked about for generations. I read new books and I read books from the late 1800's. Some of my favourites are *Pushing To The Front* by Orison Swett Marden, *Coach Wooden* by Pat Williams, and T*he 5 Levels of Leadership* by John Maxwell. My favourite fiction book, by a landslide, is *East of Eden* by John Steinbeck.

Almost A Daily Sacrifice

Today, I wake up about 4:15am and I read. It's proven to be a magnificent way to get my brain warmed up and ready to brainstorm, write, or get ready for the day ahead. A couple years ago, even the slightest inclement of getting up hours before sunrise to read of all things would have melted my brain. Of course, it has turned into one of my best disciplines concerning my learning and strengthening my mind.

What would have been once considered a sacrifice beyond comprehension has blended into a daily ritual. Well, almost a daily ritual. If I've had a late night writing or while on a date with my wife I will allow my body to rest if it wants too, but usually it doesn't. It has become extremely gratifying to fall out of bed into a good book.

What Do I - In My Infinite Wisdom - Think You Should

The books you read should always make you think. They should challenge your thoughts and beliefs. They should teach you new things. They should open you to new ideas and opportunities. I list a number of books in the resources section that will get your reading list started.

Jim Rohn, the great business philosopher, was the first person to ever teach me how important it was to read and read often. His DVD presentation, *How To Have Your Best Year Ever,* changed my thinking and ultimately my life. One of my favourite quotes from Jim Rohn was, "Miss a meal if you have to, but don't miss a book." That quote sounded crazy to me at first, but over time I've come to understand the wisdom and truth in that statement.

My great-grandpa and both my grandpa's were all avid

readers. They never fell into the trap of television like so many people do today. Reading good books keeps your mind sharp and strong, and to live a long life with independence your mind has to be working properly.

My books are gold to me. I'm very selfish when it comes to letting people borrow my books. I mark them up, bend the pages, and write thoughts in them. I have conversations with them. I always go back and refer to the books that have left the greatest impact on me.

As my curiosity and actionable reading has grown, I now finish every book I start; unless it is absolute garbage, and I have bumped into a few of those. I can now have two or three books on the go. Not at the same time, of course. That would be the ultimate for me. But since I can't read three books at once my general plan is to have a book I read in the morning, one for reading throughout the day, and one right next to my bed to read until I'm ready to fall asleep - fiction for the most part so my brain doesn't go haywire with thoughts and ideas.

John Wooden, the great UCLA basketball coach, and who has been named the greatest sports coach of all time, was a ferocious reader. He was a student of history, poetry, and great literature. Coach Wooden lived by a series of seven creeds. Number five on his list was, "Drink Deeply from Good Books."

Coach Wooden, like Jim Rohn, has taught me so much about life and the importance of books. In Pat Williams book, *Coach Wooden - The 7 Principles That Shaped His Life and Will Change Yours,* he writes:

> *Books are inexhaustible sources of knowledge and wisdom about life, the human condition, the world around us, history, philosophy,*

and more. In books, we find the lives of great leaders, successful entrepreneurs, brilliant thinkers, and people of action and accomplishment. Through the magic of books, we can experience thousands of lives, visit thousands of places, time travel through history, and explore an infinite array of ideas. Scottish literary historian Gilbert Highet said that books are not "lumps of lifeless paper, but minds alive on the shelves. From each of them goes out its own voice...and just as the touch of a button on our set will fill the room with music, so by taking down one of these volumes and opening it, one can call into range the voice of a man far distant in time and space, and hear him speak to us, mind to mind, heart to heart."

Reading from good books and taking the time to study and understand them will change your life. You will develop your own philosophies on how to live better and you will develop mental armour for the challenging times.

Personally, ever since I began to dive into good books my mindset on life has been rapid to evolve. I understand that failure is a part of success. I understand that it takes commitment and an iron will to create your success. You can't legitimately go through the motions and stay comfortable and hope that opportunity will find you.

The Old Stuff Helps Today

There are simple laws to success that have been written about for hundreds of years; hard work and self-discipline being the main laws. Learning about people who caused change in the past will help you understand how they experienced and conquered it. Don't just read the freshest paper that's hit the bookshelf. Read and treasure the old books. One of my favourite books, *Pushing To The Front* by Orison Swett Marden, was originally published in 1896. It's a book that I believe, should be mandatory reading for everybody.

Reading has taught me patience and I've developed into a much better thinker. Training my brain for a minimum of an hour a day - sometimes two or three - has given my mind the same benefits as training my body every day. I'm stronger, tougher, more versatile, more efficient, and healthier.

The most common excuse when it comes to reading - just like exercising - is the lack of time. Trust me, I used to say the same thing. Waking up at 4:15am to make sure I get my hour of reading in every day wasn't a joyful process at the start. I was given strange looks from friends when I told them what I do at a time they are most likely entering their final REM period. I was even starting to question my intensity - or insanity - about it. Without a doubt, though, the looks people give you are hilarious when you mention that you schedule 4:15am reading sessions for yourself.

How Can You Find More Time to Read?

Unfortunately, the only true answer is sacrifice. Whether it be getting up earlier, making sure you bring a book with you everywhere you go, reducing your social internet time, not watching every reality television show that's on, not watching television until you have read for an hour, or whatever the choice may be, a sacrifice needs to happen. We all have busy lives and we all have the ability to sacrifice for positive change.

As I've already mentioned, I schedule in my reading. I recommend you do too. Reading is that important. Don't take reading for granted. Don't say that you'll just start the book tomorrow because you really have to watch the new crime fighting show or because your friend wants to go out for coffee and gossip. The greatest leaders and thinkers of our time tell us that reading is a crucial part to success. This book and my life is about teaching people how to live marvellously fulfilling lives filled with wonder and great experiences.

Andy Andrews, best-selling author and world famous speaker, has said, "I've sat with kings and dined with poets, eavesdropped on history's most significant conversations and danced with ideas that forever changed me — all because I picked up a book." What a great way to view looking at words on paper. If we all took that approach to reading then it would be much easier to pick up a good biography or a book on leadership.

They Were Once Seen As Treasures

John Fitzgerald Kennedy (JFK) was an avid reader. During his youth, he was always too ill to play games with the other kids so he would read non-stop. In the old days books were considered treasures. I really believe we need to start shifting our mindset back to that. Television, the Internet, and phones are now major parts of our daily consumption, but I'd have to argue that you just can't get out of them what you can from excellent book that can nourish your life.

When Thurlow Weed, a New York newspaper publisher and politician in the 1800's, was a boy he heard of a book that a distant neighbour had that was of interest to him. He started off barefoot in the snow and hiked for miles until he arrived at the house of the book's keeper. The people consented to letting him borrow the book, but only if it was returned in the same condition. He walked back home too happy to even notice the snow on his feet.

Today, people stand outside a store battling weather of all kinds for hours - sometimes days - so they can be the first to get the latest phone or video game. The only books to my knowledge to receive that array of hype have been the Harry Potter books. Now, I have to be honest, and say that I've never read any of the Harry Potter books and probably never will, but it is nice to see one book getting that sort of desperate attention. It means some children - and closet Harry Potter adult fans - are reading and that's a start.

Where Are Your Priorities?

Every year, people spend hundreds of dollars on things that won't necessarily make them better. The latest phone is cool, but if it's not making your body or mind stronger then is it really necessary to have it? People often tell me they don't have enough money to be buying books all the time, but they have huge televisions and the latest $500 dollar phone.

Most of my money goes towards books. Since I've made that shift I've seen gigantic improvements in my mind and self-fulfillment. It feels great to make time, sit down with a book, and learn. I've fallen into the video game trap. That horrid spell when you start playing and before you can blink your night has passed you by. It was fun, but when I put down the controller I couldn't help but think how much time was wasted accomplishing nothing real.

You must, under any circumstances, put reading into your priorities of daily happenings. If you don't, then it could cost you dearly on living your very best life. The remote control and the nonchalant attitude of 'just seeing what's on' will win practically every time.

Our Mind Needs A Breaks Too

Like our body, our mind needs a break as well. That's where movies come into play for myself. I love movies. My number one favourite is Rocky. My wife and I enjoy relaxing by watching a flick at home or heading down to the theatre. In the last while, though, I've even become picky about what I want to see and have gravitated towards shows that are about great people in history, inspirational, or comedies. So don't get me wrong, television, movies, and video games can all have their place, but reading good books must always take priority.

Along the same lines of thinking comes the difference between being comfortable and uncomfortable; searching for instant gratification or delayed gratification. As I said at the beginning of this chapter, I used to hate reading and the reason was because I felt I was too slow of a reader. In reality, I was impatient and wanted to be the fastest reader alive so I could crush book after book. The true reason for that impatience boiled down to my immediate desire for gratification. Taking time to absorb and dig into a book felt like a waste of time. Wondering whether or not the book would be of value to me was enough to prevent my hands from opening it.

The Search For The Uncomfortable

When I operated my own fitness blog I wrote a two part series entitled, *The Search for The Uncomfortable*. The short articles can give insight to every part of life when dealing with that nasty discomfort that prevents progress and learning.

> **The Search for the Uncomfortable Part 1**
>
> We search and accept 'comfort' every single day. We generally love being comfortable because, well... uncomfortable sucks. A lot of the times being uncomfortable gives you feelings of anxiousness and a gigantic knot in your gut that won't go away.
>
> When we don't want to do something our mind will instantly agree with us, and attempt to find every minuscule reason out there, to keep us from doing that something.
>
> If you pay attention and notice the people around you will find that the people who accept and thrive with the uncomfortable get the results that the people who cave with the uncomfortable keep dreaming about.
>
> Exercise, for example, is uncomfortable. It causes discomfort in the muscles and it can leave you struggling for breath. Some people accept and actually love that feeling. Most people don't. It's the people who accept that feeling and force themselves into it that get the results that people are envious about.

The same goes with sports. As a college athlete it can really suck to get up at 5:30am for a 6:00am lift than an afternoon practice and then a full night of studying or homework. The thought will continue to enter your thoughts throughout the night thinking, "man, I don't want to get up in the morning." The successful athletes, the one's that are striving for greatness, will never let those thoughts win, however. I don't necessarily feel pumped about waking up every day at 4:15am, but I do because it's what I need to do to make progress on my goals.

Take a look at marketing and what we usually purchase. Usually if we buy something it's for comfort reasons (the big television, the plate of fries, etc.).

But does comfort actually make us happy?

The Search for the Uncomfortable Part 2

Does being comfortable really make us happy?

I'd have to argue that being comfortable all the time leave us with an empty feeling satisfaction...but definitely not happy overall.

I've had days where I was looking forward so much to an easy, do nothing, sort of day. You know those days, right? You work your ass off for a few weeks and you're just craving a day off with no responsibilities and no pressure. Let me tell you that I take full advantage if those days come around...even still.

My comfort days have changed, though. They used to mean lying of a couch and watching movies or random shows all day. A big nap or two mixed in there always tends to happen and the thought of preparing and cooking meals are, well... out of the question.

Today, they tend to do more with reading and writing or going for a hike or something. Sometimes my comfort days blend into what I used to find uncomfortable...like writing and using my brain to think about things to write. For me, that's a good thing because it means I'm ready for the next level of 'uncomfortable' so I can keep getting better.

Now back to my first type of comfort days though. The one's with television and crappy food. I enjoyed those days but at the end of those days I felt like I'd just wasted it. I hated that feeling which is why I am happy I am strong enough now to actually do work or be active on days where I have nothing scheduled or nothing due.

But being comfortable and continually searching to be comfortable doesn't make you happy...it leaves you empty.

Learning something new takes a great deal of effort and the thought of all that work gives feeling of discomfort. Mastering that new skill, however, brings you happiness and a feeling of true success.

Never even trying that new skill to avoid the time and effort it would take to master it leaves you with eventual feelings of regret and unhappiness.

The instant gratification we all search for typically has a negative long-term affect on us. Delayed gratification – working hard on something and improving everyday – gives us continual challenges and the satisfaction of progress… which leads to lasting happiness.

Instant gratification (comfortable) leaves us eating chips, watching too much television, and not doing the exercise.

Delayed gratification (sometimes uncomfortable) has us eating our vegetables, reading more books, and doing the exercise, because we not just want to get healthier and smarter…we actually do it.

Avoid Instant Gratification

We must do our best to tame the hidden desires of instant gratification when it comes to our health, fitness, and learning. It's challenging, because we are creatures of comfort, and we are in general most comfortable doing things that are lazy and not productive. We also love anything that makes our tastes buds come alive or that satisfies our need for a quick hit of sugar.

There are, however, some people out there who absolutely love eating healthy and are extremely active all the time - mainly people from the older generation - and that's awesome, but the fact is most people are not like that. Most people are drones in a world where they just listen and do what they are told and that's sad. It's also what's caused our deep insecurities as a society. It's what causes us to keep pace with the Jones' next door and have the new car and the expensive flooring.

Instant gratification blocks us from drawing our sword on the battle of self. On everything from taking the first step forward on our path of change - real, progressive, positive change.

Search For The Truth In The Words You Are Reading

Ernest Hemingway said in his book, *A Moveable Feast*, "I would stand and look out over the roofs of Paris and think, 'Do not worry. You have always written before and you will write now. All you have to do is write one true sentence. Write the truest sentence that you know.' So finally I would write one true sentence, and then go on from there. It was easy then because there was always one true sentence that I knew or had seen or had heard someone say."

In my opinion, all good fiction has truth behind it. The story may have been created, but the message and people have not been. I believe you would find this to be true with most of the best writers who have ever graced a sheet of paper with their words courtesy of lead from a pencil, ink from a pen, or the hard punches on a typewriter. Fantasy can have it's place, but shouldn't be a large part of your library.

I've argued in the past that the reader's form of instant gratification is fiction. I've already quoted Jim Rohn in this book and I will advise you now there will be more to come. I once heard him say, "Some people claim that it is okay to read trashy novels because sometimes you can find something valuable in them. You can also find a crust of bread in a garbage can, if you search long enough, but there is a better way." I used to label all of fiction into that quote. Today, I have come to understand that he wasn't necessarily lumping all fiction into one category. There is without question a lot of 'trash' out there on the bookshelves - both fiction and non-fiction - but I'm confident you can tell the difference and stick to good literature.

Carry The Courage to Challenge Yourself

Read books that challenge you, that make you think, and that can make you better. Read books that not only deal with self-help, but also books that teach you about history and how the world works. Learning about the world is critical. This wasn't a notion I have always believed, however.

My old business coaches, who helped me run and develop my fitness business, used to preach that I should avoid watching or reading the news. It was all too negative and would prevent me from being positive and focused on my work. It made sense at first - without any critical thinking on my part - so I believed them. I remember times it would take everything in my power to look at the front page of the newspaper because I wanted to check the sports scores and had to avoid glimpsing at anything negative. How ridiculous is that?

I can honestly say, I don't think avoiding the news helped or hampered me at all. You hear boatloads of negative things everyday anyways. It all boils down to one thing: choice. Choose to let it affect you, or choose to let in not; simple, to the point and effective. It's not complicated, it's just hard.

So learn about what is going on in the world today. If you're tough mentally it won't affect your day-to-day progress. The threat of recession won't cause you to panic. The latest diet pill won't cause you to jump off the couch and drive to your doctor so you can create your happiness with a pill. Maybe it will nudge you into local politics because you are tired of the poor leadership that it is currently under. There are many possibilities as to how the news can affect you, but I just caution you to choose your decisions with a critical and thoughtful mind.

The Power of Choice

Like everything we do or don't do in our lives, it's all a choice. As a child that's not exactly true because we have no choice as to who raises or teaches us. The first 18 years of our lives are full of situations that we don't have a choice in what we do, whether it was to go to school or go to certain events. We always had - and have - the choice of how we react, of course, and as a youngster myself once, I understand that overreactions are a necessary part of growing up. I will never live down wearing red sweat pants and a light grey Arizona sweatshirt to a family portrait when I was 11 because I didn't want to go home and change. My mullet was rocking too. Maybe the red sweats were appropriate.

As an adult we have a choice in everything we do. Whether we choose to believe that or not is up to us. Some of this is culture dependent but in North America we choose who we want to be in a relationship with, what we do for work, who we hang out with, how we spend our time, who we vote for, who to listen to, who to believe, and a wide variety of other things, including what books we read.

One of the things I miss most about coaching and playing baseball was all the bus travel. I missed the airplane travel too but there was something about the bus that I loved. Half the team would be sleeping or watching the movie that was playing on the tiny screens. A few would be doing homework, while some would be playing cards and gambling their meal money. I have lost plenty of meal money during many long road trips. It was - to me - the perfect time to just sit, relax, think, write, and read.

How Reading Helped My Anxiety and Depression

When you're a young kid and doctors hand you a bunch of pills to ingest that will 'help' your issues, you just listen. I did, for about three months. Then I started to critically think, which isn't just rare for a young kid but unfortunately for a lot of people. I started to learn about my problems and experimented with ways to help me overcome them. It was reading that was the catalyst for me ripping through the tight plastic bag that always seemed to be suffocating me on a daily basis. Reading gave me ideas and strategies. And sometimes even gave me hope when times weren't looking very good at all.

Reading changed my life and I would argue that by reading good books that inspire you to explore more of what's out there and what we are about as human beings, then your life can change also. But reading is just the start. Reading will give you the ideas, but to really take your life to another level you need a next step. A step that is essential, a step that challenges me on a daily basis, and a step that takes courage. Let's talk about that now.

CHAPTER FIVE

BE AGGRESSIVE

"I learned that courage was not the absence of fear, but the triumph over it. The brave man is not he who does not feel afraid, but he who conquers that fear." - Nelson Mandela

"Inaction breeds doubt and fear. Action breeds confidence and courage." - Dale Carnegie

"Take the first step in faith. You don't have to see the whole staircase, just take the first step." - Dr. Martin Luther King Jr.

You can read every single word in this book and agree completely with all of it, however, it will mean nothing unless you take action on it. Generally, the reason that action is a hard thing to accomplish is because of fear. The fear of failing, the fear of doubt, the fear of what others will say, the fear of what family will think, etc.

When Winston Churchill reflected on the subject of fear he said, "When I look back on all these worries, I remember the story of the old man who said on his deathbed that he had had a lot of trouble in his life, most of which had never happened."

How real is your fear? That's the question you need to come to grips with. Will your actions change things? Hopefully, that's why you're doing something, isn't it? Sometimes taking action will not leave you with a desired result and I think we can just boil that down to this being life and unfortunately we will not always get what we want. But I think taking steps forward will always lead to forward progress most of the time and those are pretty good odds. Will some people not believe in you prevent your forward movement? Most likely. Should those people be worth your time to begin with? That's entirely up to you and the strength of your belief in the actions you are taking.

A Lot Of Questions And A Lot Of Answers

There are a lot of questions and answers you can give and argue about but that's a waste of time. You need to evaluate every fear that scorches into your journey and determine how big of a factor they should be. People who change their life will inevitably change their surrounding life, as well. What I mean is if someone is addicted to drugs or alcohol and they decide to get sober, that personal change will bring about changes to their surrounding life. Where they go, who they hang out with, etc.

The thing that really puzzles me is when people honestly know that they need to change and accept they want a better life, why they never do anything about it. They just sit there and hope that one day the change will materialize out of thin air. They are strangled by fear from what people will think of them or how people might hate them for it.

I was a victim of fear and it's still a battle to this day - far less then years ago, but it will always be an enemy. I used to try and cling onto things whether it was for fear of loss or fear of uncertainty. I used to be scared that people would hate me for saying what I thought or for screwing something up. I used to think people would think I'm stupid for trying to run my own business when a nice cozy job with a salary was sitting right in front of me - a lot did, in fact. I was confident that people wouldn't listen to me because of my age.

I remember wanting to write for a long time. I have always enjoyed it. When I finally grew enough courage to write some articles and put them online I was nervous. When I received my first email that didn't agree with what I had written I was crushed. I wanted to tear down the article so nobody else could ever see it. I had received numerous emails complimenting my work, but that didn't matter once I became consumed with the disapproving reader. It took me a few weeks before I was ready to publish another article. After a while, it began to not bother me so much when I opened my inbox and a dissatisfactory email was waiting for me. I was building my thick skin that was blocking the negativity from affecting me.

Today, I take action very aggressively. A couple years ago I took massive action and shut down my business to pursue coaching college baseball - a job where I only made $500 a month. That decision, though it didn't turn out from a baseball perspective, helped me colossally in my journey with writing. The move got me onto Vancouver Island and earned me a head coaching position for a collegiate summer baseball team. While coaching that summer I picked up my first ever professional writing job. Coaching took up a lot of time with traveling and organizing but always wanting to stay busy this writing job was a great learning experience. Now I live in Victoria, BC, one of the most beautiful cities in all of Canada. Fear will always enter your mind. Reacting in a progressive fashion and overcoming uncertainty will take you on a highway that you've only dreamed about.

My Inspiration. Who is Yours?

There were times during that move when doubt crossed me and I pondered, was this really the right decision? To shut down my fitness business and move halfway across the country so I could lose a lot money every month?

Every time I had doubts like that it helped that my wife - who also risked by moving with me and having to start fresh and quit a very good career - was always there to support me and believe in my dreams. She is the love of my life and I don't think I can ever repay her for the love and support she gives me on a daily basis. She has been an inspiration for me ever since our eyes locked the first time we met before I was about to destroy her with my charity bootcamp routine at her coaching session with her running clients.

When she moved to be with me after resigning from her job she not only had to find a job in her field but also restart from the ground up. She started at $12 an hour when just a couple months earlier her time was worth $60 an hour minimum. She started her own running business and within four weeks of moving had her first client. Within three weeks at her main job she was already seen as one of the big guns and - even though still grossly underpaid - was getting a full clientele and actually creating opportunities to help the organization.

Every time I feel a little off about anything I just look at her and see the great work she is doing and is crushing fear and aggressively pursuing her profession and what she wants to do. I feel privileged every day to be able to witness it and I am lucky to be a part of it.

In Search of Fearlessness

When I battled depression it was easy to see the world with negative eyes and get lost in my little bubble of inaction. It was easy to blame and easy to make excuses about why I couldn't do this or couldn't do that. Looking back, it is disheartening some of the things I never took a chance on because I was worried what people would think.

I worked hard and got my mind right and you can imagine what some people thought when I told them that I was leaving to move across the country for a severe pay cut. But I didn't care. I was doing what I knew I was supposed to do and the sacrifice of no money was just a challenge to see how much that goal really meant to me.

Mahatma Gandhi said about fearlessness, "One cannot follow truth or love so long as one is subject to fear. As there is at present a reign of fear in the country, meditation on and cultivation of fearlessness have a particular importance. Hence its separate mention as an observance. A seeker after truth must give up the fear of parents, caste, government, robbers, etc., and he must not be frightened by poverty or death."

We are all affected by fear, even Gandhi was. There are differences between the people who change the world and the people who don't, the people who are successful in their lives and the people who aren't. The difference is their action through fear.

Living life aggressively doesn't mean yelling, screaming, and forcing your way. It means acknowledging and accepting the fear. It is having the courage to move through that fear and take action on your thoughts and opinions; not letting people bend your will.

The Haters Are Coming

Once you take action the hardest aspect starts to be surviving the array of inevitable opinion bullets that will be fired your way. Staying true to your thoughts and actions is crucial in your success and bending one way or another, because of other people who may not have your best interest in mind, will be detrimental in the long run. The haters will try and bring you down. The good thing about having haters, nevertheless, is that it means you're being successful or saying things worth talking about.

Maya Angelou, an American author and poet, wrote her definition of what a hater is as follows:

> *A hater is someone who is jealous and envious and spends all their time trying to make you look small so they can look tall.*
>
> *They are very negative people to say the least. Nothing is ever good enough! When you make your mark, you will always attract some haters...That's why you have to be careful with whom you share your blessings and your dreams, because some folk can't handle seeing you blessed...*

It's dangerous to be like somebody else…

If God wanted you to be like somebody else, He would have given you what He gave them! Right? You never know what people have gone through to get what they have.

The problem I have with haters is that they see my glory, but they don't know my story… If the grass looks greener on the other side of the fence, you can rest assured that the water bill is higher there too!

We've all got some haters among us! People envy you because you can:

Have a relationship with God
Light up a room when you walk in
Start your own business
Tell a man / woman to hit the curb (if he / she isn't about the right thing)
Raise your children without both parents being in the home

Haters can't stand to see you happy, Haters will never want to see you succeed, Haters never want you to get the victory, most of our haters are people who are supposed to be on our side. How do you handle your undercover haters?

You can handle these haters by:

1. *Knowing who you are & who your true friends are *(VERY*

IMPORTANT!!)

2. Having a purpose to your life? Purpose does not mean having a job.

3. You can have a job and still be unfulfilled. A purpose is having a clear sense of what God has called you to be. Your purpose is not defined by what others think about you.

4. By remembering what you have is by divine prerogative and not human manipulation. Fulfill your dreams!

You only have one life to live...when it's your time to leave this earth, you 'want' to be able to say, 'I've lived my life and fulfilled 'my' dreams,... Now I'm ready to go HOME! When God gives you favor, you can tell your haters, Don't look at me...Look at Who is in charge of me...'

My favourite part of Angelou's writing is: *The problem I have with haters is that they see my glory, but they don't know my story... If the grass looks greener on the other side of the fence, you can rest assured that the water bill is higher there too!*

That is what's going to eat your insides up the most. The haters will see your success and call you 'lucky' or demean the process they think you took to get where you are. They are going to make snarky comments and they will try to knock you down a notch if they can.

It happened to me with my college baseball career. I was pretty successful and played some of the highest level of college ball you can play. There were always people from my hometown who tried to discredit things to make my accomplishments seem not that important. It would not necessarily bother me, but sometimes it was aggravating listening to people try and degrade your accomplishments. My first thought was always, "You don't know how hard I worked to get to Division I." My next thought would certainly be a little crueler, "People who have never done anything significant in their lives sure do get envious easily."

That might not have been the most heart-warming thought that has ever crossed my mind, but in my eyes it was authentic and true. You must recognize the more success you find the more people are going to carry and share their opinions of you and your actions. There will be incredible amounts of positive opinions, but understand there will be your fair share of negative opinions also.

They will observe the outside view - the results - but they won't take a good hard look at the sacrifice and commitment you made to create the results you did. I will tell you right now that most people will never understand the true effort you are actually putting into your life - never. Haters are just part of the territory. The bigger the mission the more haters you'll have. Oh well, they are the people who are holding themselves back.

Should You Please Everyone?

Colin Powell, the 65th United States Secretary of State, said, "Trying to get everyone to like you is a sign of mediocrity." Sometimes that's a tough idea to accept. Growing up we all experienced phases of friendships. When you were really young everybody was a friend. Then as you grew older little cliques started to form. Once you got to high school you just wanted to be in the cool kids group, and in college you might have agreed to perform stupid activities to be accepted into a fraternity. I can honestly say I've never understood, or had the urge, to join a fraternity. We always wanted to be accepted and to some extent that is still happening in your life today.

The danger, when you are trying to be liked by everybody, is you will shape your views around theirs. It is like having a tug-of-war battle in your mind about what ideas you agree or disagree with. One person tells you his or her opinion and you agree. Then another person comes in and gives the opposite view, you nod and say, "yeah, that makes sense." The problem is you are not making an original decision for yourself because of your fear that the other person will disagree with you and potentially not like you because of that.

It has always been a personal challenge to not care what other people think of my actions and opinions. As I learned playing college baseball, when you start winning awards or do incredibly well, there will be people jumping out of the woodworks to try and make it sound like you didn't deserve them or are 'lucky' because of natural talent.

I have always admired professional coaches due to the outlandish amount of criticism they draw from reporters and sports fans on a near daily basis. In the world of sports everybody seems to know everything. With the advantage of hindsight they are always quick to blast the coach for a decision that didn't work out. Most coaches say that you just become immune to it and that's the simple fact of it. When I was head coach of a summer collegiate baseball team I learned how to let opinions bounce off me as they were thrown at me.

My wife would always call me after games and let me know what the announcers were saying about my decisions. Of course, they were usually while we were on the road so you can't expect them to treat you like you are a bright guy. I always laughed and once I told a reporter after he asked me about a decision that ended up going wrong, "at least I was out there trying to create something while it seems like most people are judging with the power of hindsight." When you leave yourself open to be judged you will be judged. You must have the courage to open yourself up and let the judgers judge. You would rather be a doer than a judger. It's an infinitely better way to live.

A Slow and Brutal Torment

Most people are great at tormenting themselves until they hit a place I would call rock bottom. That point when life - or a specific area of life - gets so bad and helpless they don't care anymore and decide to make a change. A change that in retrospect could have happened long ago to avoid the bottom of the pit. A change that would have saved them years of hardship, struggle, and unhappiness.

I was a kid who let things eat me up in a slow and painful manner. Whether it was because of an offhand comment by somebody towards me or somebody disagreeing with something I did. I would try to forget or let it pass but most of the time it never did. I have always been an independent thinker and that can prove to be a little hard during your teenage years when being accepted is a large part of the self-esteem domain.

One day after a class while in high school, myself and a couple of my buddies had Vaseline all over the locks on our lockers. It turned the lock dial into a slick mess. We found out who it was - a girl whose locker was right beside mine - and why she did it. She was not a number one fan of athletes. Well, my buddies decided they were going to move lockers. I decided to wear out the storm. Why? I don't know.

Day after day my lock would be covered and I acted like I didn't even notice. Soon enough the torment intensified enough that I started to retaliate with my own concoctions on her locker. It built up to glue being used. Then, after a couple weeks of frustration, it finally got to me; I snapped. I waited for this girl and we started screaming at one another. I don't remember what was said but a truce was formed. There were never anymore issues. Anyhow, the entire situation was something that could have been dealt with immediately.

That was not the last time my crawling frustration led to explosive actions. In college, our team felt that there was a communication issue, but it was apparent none of us wanted to say anything about it to the coaches. Instead we complained to each other about it. It bothered us, but when nobody stepped up to have a private meeting, it was more our fault than the coaches.

One day, a communication error happened again and myself along with three of my other teammates showed up an hour late to practice. We just jumped right in and at the completion of practice my coach gathered the four of us together and demanded, "Why the hell were you late?" I barely let him finish the question before I became enraged and we were almost nose-to-nose screaming at each other. Most of the team was still there and stood in shock watching this fiasco. What turned out to be the most comical part of this scream match was when he told me to get an answering machine and I yelled back, "I can't afford an answering machine, you get me an answering machine." Ah, the magic of what comes out of your mouth when unplanned screaming happens.

I was pissed off - as you could probably tell - and after a couple minutes of shouting back and forth at each other, my coach left for hitting practice and I stayed to do the ten sprints we had been punished to run. I did not exactly run them full force and was still obviously furious as our assistant coach kept telling me to relax and that it was already forgotten about.

We went to our hitting practice and there was noticeable tension between the coach and I. After a few drills my coach came by and tried to tell a joke. I responded with an emotionless comment, but the fight was over and we could move on.

We actually became good friends after that incident. In our team meetings he would always ask and value my opinion about the vibe around the team. The issue, of course, is that whole crazy situation could have been avoided completely if just one person stepped up and went into our coaches office one day and just said, "hey, some of us are feeling that communication isn't the best right now and I was wondering if we could talk about it?"

That's it. Everybody, including myself, failed and it built into an insane blow out.

Take Care of The Issues As Fast As You Can

You have to be aggressive and take care of issues before they get out of hand, potentially crippling you and your progress.

One of my favourite stories regarding taking care of a

problem before it hurts the chemistry of your team is the story of how Ron Singleton got fired from the San Francisco 49ers. He was one of the best players on the 49ers and wanted more money. Singleton hired an agent and began the process of renegotiation. Bill Walsh, both the General Manager and the Head Coach, didn't agree with Singleton's demands.

Walsh was in a tough place because Singleton was a crucial part of the team. Not satisfied, Singleton started to bring race into the picture saying they would not negotiate seriously or give him more money because he was African American. Singleton was also verbally abusive towards some staff members and that was strongly against Walsh's philosophy and rules for the team.

After yet another unproductive contract session, Singleton was irritated and went to the locker room and started saying some nasty things about Walsh and the organization. Word got back to Walsh about Singleton's outrage and without hesitation got on the phone with the team's public relations person. Walsh asked him to go to Singleton's locker and clear it out.

Under an hour later, the box full of Singleton's clothes and materials had been dropped off on the front steps of his home. He had been released.

Tighten The Wheels Before They Fall Off

When you are a fitness professional it is guaranteed you will become a blend of a psychiatrist and guru of the pushup. There were numerous times when the wheels looked as if they were starting to fall off for some clients. Whether it was personal problems, money problems, relationship problems, work problems, or anything really, life challenged them - as it will all of us - and forced them to make a decision and choose how to deal with the situation.

Let me share a story about this from my training days. I was training a young lady in her early twenties. She was an early morning client and one of the hardest workers I have ever trained. She would always demand more of herself and it was a pleasure to train her. One morning she came in, started doing her foam rolling and you could tell just by asking how her night had been that something was up. She acknowledged something was bothering her but assured me it was nothing. She put on a tough face and went to work. Twenty minutes into the workout we started doing kettle bell swings. She struggled with them; she usually didn't. I immediately halted the session and sat her down. I told her that whatever was going on was putting her at risk of injury because she was not focusing on the exercise.

She immediately broke down and started talking about issues affecting her the past few days. We talked for half an hour, solved some problems, and worked on getting a different viewpoint on the day. She even left with a bit of a smile. To be safe and productive - and that has happened with many clients over the years - we had to get to the bottom of the issues and work at solving the problem. That is more important then another set of pushups, squats, swings, or anything physical.

As a coach it is my responsibility to handle problems before they escalate into substantial problems that can harm the person or the team. In your life, you must approach problems that are brewing or have already come to the surface as fast as possible. It will be uncomfortable, but in the end it will be worth it. So if you feel that the wheels are starting to loosen, take the time to look at the problem and tighten the wheels back up before they cause real damage.

Make Sure Your Friends Are Actual Friends

This has always been an interesting topic to me. Who are my true friends and who is just 'hanging' out? I recognized early on I made friends because I was one of the better athletes in school. If you can help your team win during recess you make friends. I had many friends until I started high school. Then they dwindled down to about three. I didn't party so that caused me to lose a few. I was a quiet fella and there were no longer opportunities to win a football game during recess, so that weeded out the rest. I was okay with it. I never felt the need to have a large clan of friends; it seemed too busy.

My need for aloneness, I believe, stemmed from the melancholy that was creeping into my personality in my mid-teens. I have always been a reflective person with a high-speed mind. The conversations I have with myself are more than enough to keep me occupied. I am serious about that last sentence too. I have heard that it is fine to take to yourself, the problem is if you answer back. Thank goodness I haven't answered back yet.

I'm very picky with friendships. I don't like baggage (who does?) and I believe drama for the sake of drama is borderline psychotic. Spending hours complaining in a coffee shop to each other is viral and wasteful. If your friends aren't aligned or supportive of your dreams then I would suggest you run away - fast.

The word 'selfish' gets a lot of negative press and I understand why. When a person is selfish, they are strictly concerned with their own needs and have no remorse for the consequences on other people. However, you have to have a little selfishness in you when it comes to friends. Being selfish here does not mean you use your friends for your own personal gains. Being selfish with relationships means you get rid of friends that have a negative impact on you so they don't stop your progress and weigh you down. Negative people need to stay away from you. Drama hunters need to vanish into their forest of neediness. Constant borrowers need to start doing the work themselves. If they are your true friends they will seek advice, help whenever they can, and not let you settle for less than you can be.

A true friend does not like you for who you are. A true friend challenges and encourages you to reach the greatness they know you are capable of. Have you ever thought that maybe your friend is happy that you are unhappy or living a mediocre life because it gives them permission to be mediocre themselves? Interesting idea, isn't it? Having a core group of true friends can bring about dramatic change in your attitude and priorities when it comes to relationships. When an acquaintance - a friend you hangout with, but just to gossip and waste time with- asks you for a favour but you don't have the time to do it, you can easily say no. If they get so mad it hurts your acquaintanceship (did you ever think you would see that word actually used in a book?) with that other person, then how close were you in the first place? If you can help great, but if you can't or simply would rather do other things then the power is all yours.

Never rely on other people. It's a dangerous game. It declares less personal responsibility and more neediness. When I was battling my depression at its worst I hung out with people who liked to drink and party. It was a release for me to run away from my realities and spend time in this fun bubble that had zero affect on fixing my real problems. I had a lot of friends. There would always be at least one of them wanting to do something and be my excuse for forgetting about fixing myself - or studying for exams for that matter - for another day. When I hit rock bottom on a bus in Evansville, Indiana I made some changes. Not in dramatic fashion, but very analytical. Who was helping me? Who was taking advantage? Who gave me thoughtful advice about actions now and how they could play out in the future?

Before I knew it I had an invisible 'true' friends list and an acquaintances list. Nobody knew who was on what. There was not a physical copy and they did not know I was making any type of list. This also sounds extremely harsh and maybe it is, but it was the right move. Helping break out of my struggles meant I needed to surround myself and talk to positive influences. When I say positive influences I don't mean people who will just spout happy, feel good answers. I mean real answers with thought backing them up. If their answers hurt your feelings then it was okay because you have chosen them on a list of people you trust. Trust is the key to all of this. Your acquaintances advice might be good every once in awhile, but from my experience they never even give much advice because they are so busy wanting to tell you how crazy and awful their own life is and need you to feel sorry for them.

Friends are a crucial part of life, but the more friends you have does not necessarily make things better. Find friends who make you a better person, who are inline with your lifestyle, and who challenge you to be your best. When I focused on my friends who would support me and have open-minded talks about life, my life began to soar.

Having Fun is Necessary

You do not have to be type A personality to live an aggressive life. Your days and actions should not engulf you with the curse of being uptight either. It is freeing to understand that it is okay to laugh at yourself. There is no immediate laughter about being depressed and anxious all the time. Now that I have evolved past those torments I can comfortably tell people about when I used to toss my dinner up in a wastebasket while talking on the phone to people. Or when I had to throw up out of a moving car - while I was driving - because the anxiety of what I was about to do or what had just happened was so overwhelming. I can now laugh at myself over those experiences.

I can tell you that one way to avoid anxiety is to knock yourself out cold and proceed the rest of the day with not only a concussion but stitches in your head and dried up blood caking your hair.

One sunny summer morning while I was playing in the Northwoods League - a summer collegiate baseball league - I tried to wake my sister up by catapulting myself on her. My hometown just received an expansion team that summer and I was asked to play for them. So I got the chance to play high-level college baseball during the summer and live at home when we were not on the road. It was a once in a lifetime situation so I took full advantage of it. On this particular morning I was feeling full of energy, had a busy schedule planned with some media appearances and then, of course, the game that night.

I decided it would be a fun idea to ruin my sisters sleep - makes sense, right? - so I started off in a full sprint down the hallway and just so happened to time my jump perfectly that my head hit the top of the doorway brutally hard. The last thing I remember was falling as my world turned to black. I awoke on my stomach. When I raised my head and my vision defogged all I saw was a pool of blood under me. With an alarmed sensation shooting through me I gave a panicked look over to the bed where my sister - now awake - had sat up with confused and shocked attention. I had accomplished my mission, just not how I intended.

I rushed to the bathroom where my reflection in the mirror revealed my current condition. I looked like I had just competed in a barbwire match and had been repeatedly smoked in the head by a chair. My face was covered by flowing blood. I then threw up. I decided it would be in my best interest to head to emergency to get stitched up. I let my sister know that we had to hurry because I had an autograph signing to be at in a couple hours. When we arrived I don't know how many times I mentioned I was in a hurry because I needed to go sign my name on things. I'm confident I annoyed people enough that within 30 minutes I was stitched up and on my way home.

In my obvious concussed state I couldn't find my baseball hat so I grabbed my next best option - a black Wrangler cowboy hat. I then took the car and drove to the stadium to pick up the other players going to the autograph session. The look on their face when they saw me was priceless. We were behind schedule so I grabbed my jersey and ran back to the car. All this while I refused to acknowledge numerous pieces of advice that I should clean my face; I still had dry blood all over my hair and forehead.

The event we headed to was a cheerleading camp for about 30 girls between the ages of 7-13. Looking at a concussed baseball player with hair chalked full of dry blood hanging out from under his cowboy hat was, I am sure, scary enough. But when I joined in to dance and do the cheers with them that fear - with a blend of intrigue - was taken to a whole new level.

I always had fun at events like that. That is the reason, even though most people could argue not consciously, that I did not want to let anything prevent me from going to it. I could rest later. Every time I have a job to do I want to perform it to the best of my ability and showing up to a cheerleading event all bloodied up in a cowboy hat was the best I could do at that moment. Oh, and I didn't play that night.

Conquer Your Spare Moments

I now spend most of my time writing, while still keeping involved in the fitness industry. It is tough sometimes to look at my schedule for the day and attempt to comprehend how I will be able to complete it all. It is not necessarily about how busy you are that is the key. It is about how you spend your time when it is fully available to you; your spare moments. If your typical spare moments are spent watching television or having meaningless conversations with others then I urge you to make a change. It is fine to watch a little television and get updated on your friends lives, but just like everything else, if it is in excess then you are being wasteful with your time - your limited and precious time.

It's ridiculous to proclaim that you should take advantage of every spare moment available. Watching a movie or your favourite show are good things to do every once in awhile. The point is to not let them affect your progress. You will know if you are avoiding what you should really be doing. Working in the fitness industry, the number one excuse is lack of time. I would imagine that is the top excuse for the failure of any goal.

The unfortunate part about time, however, is that once that second has passed, it has passed forever. Never in the history of the world will you get that second back. So you should be critical on how you are spending those seconds. We have many spare moments during our days. There are the 10 minutes while the water builds to a boil. The 10 minutes while the coffee is brewing. The 10 minutes you wait while the car is warming up in the frigid morning. Our lunch breaks or mid-morning breaks. Those are all spare moments. Those 10-minute chunks add up to hours and what you do in those 10 minutes will add up as well. Whether you read, write, or exercise, for example.

Joseph Cook, who became the sixth Prime Minister of Australia, never wasted time, even during his youth. While students waited in line for breakfast talking and messing around with each other, Cook would turn to the big dictionary in the corner of the room and learn synonyms of words or its derivation. Even if there were only 30 seconds of waiting he would be reading.

I understand the argument is the need for rest and relaxation, to 'turn our brains off for awhile.' I understand, but we rest and are lazy to be comfortable. When is the last time being comfortable brought great progress? I would like to add that meditation or reflecting are not wastes of time. Reflection can prove to be a very uncomfortable activity and many people cannot find comfort in sitting quietly for more than a mere minute anyways. I reflect regularly. Often, I will schedule time in my day to do it. It helps because I am reflecting on how I can progress as a human being.

Orison Swett Marden said, "Waste of time means waste of energy, waste of vitality, waste of character in dissipation. It means bad companions, bad habits. It means waste of opportunities, which will never come back. Beware how you kill time, for all your future lives in it." Don't let time pass you by. I say that a lot, but it can never be said enough.

Operation Proper Rest

You might find it strange that I would now mention allowing yourself proper rest after talking about how you should be putting your open time to use, but rest is different. Let me explain. Getting a proper night sleep is important but will never always happen. Some people work well with scheduled sleep times. I work best when I go to bed when my body tells me too, but I will get up the same time every morning no matter what time I went to sleep the following night. If I get a little less sleep the night before usually my body wants to go to bed a little bit earlier the next night. With my exercise and nutrition throughout the day I never get sluggish. Every once in a while I will take a 15-20 minute nap during the afternoon but only when necessary.

Too much sleep can be hazardous. When I was in the depths of my depression I slept a lot. Every moment I could, I slept. It allowed the world to disappear for a while. I never wanted to accept the fact that the world would be the same when I awoke. I was never as alert as I could have been. As with anything, being sleepy can turn into a habit. If you are laying down sleeping or being lazy all the time than habitually you will continue to keep doing so. You can change that with a proper schedule and doing things everyday that keeps you energetic and productive. If you create good rest habits you will naturally create good action habits.

By not getting proper rest you could be headed towards an unforgiving brick wall called burnout. It can cripple you, sometimes in near permanent fashion. Dick Vermeil, head coach of the Philadelphia Eagles in the early 80's, had a sign in his office that said, "The best way to kill time is to work it to death." Vermeil almost did just that. He would sleep five nights a week in his office and only for a few hours. He then worked all day until he was exhausted. He was so relentless with his work he burnt himself out and had to quit coaching in 1982. Vermeil didn't coach again until 1997. As Vermeil told reporters, "I worked time to death until it killed me."

It took Vermeil nearly 15 years to coach again. He was so intense about coaching and winning that he never allowed himself to rest and recover when he needed it. There are times when you certainly must push through the fatigue and keep working, but it can become a very fine line to be crossing. It is one thing to take advantage of your spare moments. It is another thing to grind until you almost drop from exhaustion.

Sometimes - due to deadlines - I will have to push past fatigue to get my assignments completed. That is okay, unless I turn it into a habit. They say sleep is for the weak. I say sleep is for the people who lack passion and purpose. You have heard the eight hours of sleep per night claim and I believe that is a solid reference but it is not for everybody. It is all about what works best for you. If you were doing something that does not work best for you, then I would recommend you think about not doing that. Genius, I know.

No matter how much rest you do get, it must be enough to keep you fresh and avoid burnout. It is like building muscle. If you do not give your muscles the proper nutrition and rest then they won't grow efficiently. Likewise, if you do not allow your mind proper rest you will not have a clear head to make decisions.

Focus on Today, While Building For Tomorrow

Every day that passes is another one gone forever. We will never get it back. So my question is, why should we live that day passively? Why not live it aggressively, rest, and then do it again? We all need to start enjoying life for what it can bring us. It is about consistently and aggressively building your reserve, in all aspects of life.

What is your reserve? It is your stability in case something goes wrong. In this day and age job creation is a major topic of discussion in politics. There is no stability in the job force anymore and if you don't have a financial reserve saved up and you lose your job then you can be in serious trouble. Especially if you have to provide for your family and not just yourself. What if you hurt your knee and need surgery? The health reserve you have built with exercise and proper nutrition will help make the recovery easier than if you were out of shape.

Focus on today, while building for tomorrow. Give today everything you've got. Wake up before dawn every day and enjoy silence or dive into high-energy exercise. The choice is yours. As I have written above, rest is a big part of living life aggressively; crucial in fact. If you go too hard for too long it will just lead to burnout. Once that happens it can take days, months, and sometimes even years of productivity away from you.

When I ran my first ever (and only so far) marathon I was far too energized at the beginning of the race. When you are in a crowd of over 10,000 people on the streets of Vancouver it is pretty exciting. The build up was amazing. I had my music pumping and the vibration of the crowd was electrifying. Then the starting gun went off and I didn't move. Not because I wasn't ready, but because you have to wait for the few thousand people in front of you to start going. Once I eventually got to the starting line I took off. I felt strong. I was cutting around people and dodging the 'slow-polks'. I felt good and, if I do say so myself, I was looking good too out there cruising along.

This was the first time I had ever ran over 10km in a race atmosphere so, to be honest, I wasn't really sure what to expect since a marathon is 42.2km. This is not to say I was not prepared for the race. I trained through a group called Team in Training and raised money for The Leukemia and Lymphoma

Society. At the halfway point I still felt good. It took me two hours to run the 21.1km and for a 6'3", 215 pound guy that is pretty good. Our coaches told us to not start too fast out of the gate because - just in case we forgot - we were about to run a marathon and there is a reason people always give that advice, "It's a marathon, not a sprint."

At the halfway point I was laughing and started thinking how wrong my coach was - she also was my girlfriend, now my wife. Then it happened; a terrifying cramp in my right quad. No big deal, I thought. I walked it off and started running again. Thirty seconds later it hit me with even more tenacity. I took a swig from a gel pack to give me a little boost of energy and then I went again. About a minute later it cramped again. I walked for a while and every so often I would give running a try. Sometimes it worked, a lot of the time it did not. I started to panic and pondered the thought of actually not being capable of finishing the marathon.

Well, I absolutely was going to finish the race. I did not wake up in the freezing cold weather to run on the icy streets of Edmonton every Saturday to not finish this race. So I battled and kept going, knowing that I could not stop to rest or my day would be over.

I continued while the people I passed the first half were now starting to pass me. At the 36km mark I passed a man who looked to be in his 70's and limped like he was hurting more then I was. I walked pass him and I distinctly remember saying to myself, "At least I'm going to beat this guy."

I continued on - slowly - and worked my way to the 39km mark where Karlee was waiting to help me out for the last few kilometers. She gave me motivation and I swore back. We tried to use the momentum of the downhill portion of the bridge to get me running. It worked for a few seconds. At this point, I feel I should mention that my back, quads, knees, ankles, calves and hips were suffering like I have never felt before, so the experience was amazing let me tell you.

Somewhere around the 40km mark that 70 year old man limped by me and I almost had a seizure I was so distraught when I couldn't muster any retaliation to chase after him. The thoughts that go through your head when you are in that state are quite interesting. I have never been so eager to yell at all the lazy people just sitting there telling me I was 'almost there' and that I was 'looking good.' Bunch of liars is what they were.

As the story goes, we reached 41km and Karlee was still in a relationship with me even after some of the horrible things I am confident I blurted out. A strategy was then laid on the table. We saw an intersection 300 meters ahead and she informed me that once we got to that intersection we were going to start running. Then she would leave me to finish the race on my own. I agreed. About 20 meters from the intersection she started to pick up her pace and urged me to start my run. I screamed out, "WE AREN'T AT THE INTERSECTION YET!" She stopped and we kept walking. Ten seconds later I was off and running and finished my marathon in 5 hours and 28 minutes.

I went out of the gates too hard and didn't give myself the opportunity to rest enough at the beginning of the race and it cost me a lot of time - and pain, for that matter. I sprinted the first half causing the second half to take me nearly twice as long than the first. To be truthful, running that marathon was one of the greatest experiences of my life and I cannot thank my wife and Team in Training enough for helping me accomplish such a feat. If I were to offer any sort of advice to anyone thinking about running a marathon it would be to not only listen to your coach, but put the body glide everywhere your body rubs together - even your butt crack. Man, that was a painful couple of days.

CHAPTER SIX

BE BETTER TODAY THAN YOU WERE YESTERDAY

"Don't wish it were easier; wish you were better. Don't wish for less problems; wish for more skills. Don't wish for less challenges; wish for more wisdom." - Jim Rohn

"Every day you may make progress. Every step may be fruitful. Yet there will stretch out before you an ever-lengthening, ever-ascending, ever-improving path. You know you will never get to the end of the journey. But this, so far from discouraging, only adds to the joy and glory of the climb." - Winston Churchill

"I do not think much of a man who is not wiser today than he was yesterday." - Abraham Lincoln

"Repetition is the key to learning." - John Wooden

There are two aspects that must be discussed when talking about my journey through my battles with anxiety and depression. The first is focusing on bettering myself every single day. The second is helping someone else get better every single day.

As I mentioned in *The Reading Part* (Chapter 4), I do everything in my power to get an hour of reading in every day. It allows me to learn something new and expands my mind; whether it is a subject I am just learning or a story that I have never read. If it adds some value to my life, my family, my business, or any important part of my life then I am wiser. I am able to then also help people around me with information or advice.

There is a challenging idea towards the quest of getting better, however. Every great challenge, whether a big work project or training for a sporting event, is guaranteed to hit crossroads. This point is where it seems too hard, that results aren't consistently happening, or the end appears non-existent. It happened multiple times in the writing of this book.

Getting better every single day will prove tough and daunting at times, but that is the beauty of it. Life is not supposed to be easy. Vaulting yourself into greatness' path shouldn't be easy. It should challenge, question, give hope, build character, and create lasting change. It is the journey, after all that is important. It is the journey that forges willpower and brings a new powerful you into existence.

The act of improving every day demands persistence for the simple fact you have made the choice to no longer settle for mediocrity. It surrounds us every day. People accepting less from their lives then they are capable. My lifestyle took on a drastic overhaul while overcoming anxiety and depression. When people used to ask me how my night was, my typical response was usually, "Not bad. I just watched some television." Not that it is a bad thing every once in while, but this was my response most times. That is the answer of somebody settling for average. Obviously, there were many things I could have been doing instead of watching people critique amateur singers trying to get their 'big break.'

The Temptation Will Try To Haunt Your Life

Temptation is all around us every moment of every day. I've heard it named Mr. Resistance. It is the force out there that challenges our ability to improve or stay on course. It is the dessert of our daily actions. We know we probably shouldn't eat it but our minds convince us how damn good it is going to taste. Every time that you say 'no' to temptation it builds a layer on your willpower to stay strong when Mr. Resistance comes knocking at your door.

Bill Walsh, who is considered by many the greatest coach in the history of football, lead the San Francisco 49ers to three Super Bowl Championships in the 80's, but almost gave in to Mr. Resistance. If he had given in, football would have never remembered who he ever was. When Walsh took over the 49ers they had only won 2 games and lost 14 the previous year. Walsh came in and put into place his system for success immediately. He weeded out the players and people in management who had negative influences on his system. In that first season the 49ers had a win-loss record of 2-14. This was exactly the same as the year prior to taking over the helm. It was discouraging but it was also very encouraging when Walsh analyzed all the numbers from that year and saw how much they had actually improved from the previous year. I have read that some players called that team the best 2-14 team in league history.

With hopes high for Walsh's second year, the results rushed to the forefront with the 49ers winning the first three games of the year. The team was excited, management was excited, and 49er fans everywhere were finally realizing that maybe their team wasn't meant to always be a bottom of the barrel team. The team promptly went on an eight game losing downfall. After that eighth straight loss in Miami, Walsh boarded the plane back to San Francisco in a state of utter depression. He actually began weeping uncontrollably and the other coaches had to huddle around him so they could shield him from the players.

At one point on the flight back he decided that he would hand in his resignation the next morning. But then, as he writes in his book, along with writers Steve Jamison and Craig Walsh, *The Score Takes Care of Itself*:

> *I have tried to describe my anguish, but the words come up short. Everything I had dreamed of professionally for a quarter of a century was in jeopardy just eighteen months after being realized. And yet there was something else going on inside me, a "voice" from down deeper than the emotions, something stirring that I had learned over many years in football and, before that, growing up; namely, I must stand and fight again, stand and fight or it was all over.*

If Walsh did not show the tenacity and persistence to work through the pain of that moment he wouldn't have fought through the final five games of that year. They ended 3-2 those last games. The next year, his third as the 49ers head coach, they won the SuperBowl. If you can't tell, I am a huge Bill

Walsh fan.

Procrastination and The Grind Days

Successful people do what unsuccessful will not. A statement you've probably heard before, but one that holds true and should never leave your consciousness.

Procrastination is such a funny thing. We avoid work we know we eventually have to do, but don't really want to do, so we let it sit there until we have to do the work that we still don't want to do. This, of course, is very common and a battle most college students engaged in. It was true for myself during my first couple years in college. I used to be like every other college baseball athlete in the fact that if there was a baseball game on television, I was going to watch that before I would even think about doing any type of studying.

I also enjoyed walking to the campus bars for nights out with my friends. I had a year of my life where I could care less about school. It was when my depression and anxiety were at their worst. It got bad enough where I was taking advantage of 'drunken monkey' Thursday nights, even when I had a test early the next morning. 'Drunken monkey' nights were those glorious nights I paid $10 for a wristband and I did not have to pay another dime the rest of the night. It was all I could drink for 10 bucks. You can see for a college student how that can take priority over studying. I hated my classes. I honestly still do not agree with how our educational system is structured. It is just a waste of money taking classes that won't help get jobs or have any relevance on how to be a good human being or properly take care of yourself.

Before I get too far off track I am going to reel back into the subject of procrastination. It is the mightiest of the mighty when it comes to our personal enemies. It has the ability to cripple people, make them weak, and cause them to suffer and breakdown. It enters our brains every time we think about doing something productive that we don't necessarily want to do. It is amazing how this 'nothingness' affects our daily actions. Even the work we want to get accomplished continues to get pounded like a hammer striking a nail by thoughts of procrastination. Procrastination wants to make everything seem daunting. It pours discomfort into our bodies and we shut down, lying to ourselves that we just need another hour to relax, and then we will do what we need to do. We do this so we can feel comfortable and continue our path of mediocrity.

I wrote an article for Inside Fitness Magazine called *The Grind Days,* and I talked about the kind of days we all experience; the days we don't feel like doing anything. I talked about bodybuilders and how their lives are dedicated to the gym and they go, even they don't want to, every single day. It is the successful ones who just grind it out and work through that damper emotionless mood.

The grind days are important because they test us. They ask us if we really want what we are asking for. They challenge us to whether we actually want to put the necessary work in to achieve what we desire to achieve. The grind days suck, period! However, they are important to our true success.

Whether it is your exercise or your nutrition, whether you actually want to read or write, whether you want to clean the house or leave it messy, whether you want to have the beer or just the water, they all challenge what our standards are for ourselves. They demand us to unveil our true character and the willpower we posses. This is 'to the core stuff' I am talking about here. This is the make it or break it information. It happens every day, no matter what. You will struggle with it every day. I battle with it every day. We all do. The people who make the most progress are the ones who bare down, lock eyes with the enemy and move towards it, because no matter how hard it is pushing, you need to push back harder. Every step towards it will weaken it and before you know it you are making progress. With every victory against procrastination comes another notch in the progress belt. You need to weaken procrastinations spirit. It is not easy, but it is the only way to move forward. It does not matter if we are talking about relationships, business, health, or whatever. If you want to be a champion, if you want to strive for excellence, or if you want to change the world, you have to battle through the grind days and be relentless, because on the other side is your victory. How is that for some intense procrastination talk?

Create Your Masterpiece

Trust me, I've questioned everything I have just told you. I have wondered to myself, "Why don't I just take the job and cakewalk through life?" or "Why don't I just settle down and guarantee myself that I'll at least always be with someone?" That is, of course, the cowards way out. The more I reflected and the more I challenged myself to get better every day, the less all that average and settling down stuff made sense.

I could have settled down in a past relationship. The writing was on the wall. It was time to get married, but I pulled the plug. I did not like where my life would be heading if I committed. I am sure glad I got out of it too, because now I am married to a beautiful girl who has changed my life and supports everything I do. In the writing and coaching world, if you don't have a partner who fully understands the demands of the job it can create severe difficulties. I am grateful every day that I found Karlee and I am lucky to have her on this journey.

I could have settled down in an office job but that would have left me unsatisfied and unfulfilled. I took risks and got back into college baseball as a coach and at one point was living off of $500 a month. I did the math and I was making $1.85 an hour - and that's in 2011. That decision brought me out to Vancouver Island and took my writing to new levels. If it was not for moving to pursue coaching, my writing would have never gotten to be a priority for me. It is strange how it all worked out, but sometimes you just have to accept and love the uncommon process as it unfolds.

One of Coach John Wooden's creeds is make each day your masterpiece. In the book, *Coach Wooden*, by Pat Williams, he writes about how Coach Wooden explains what he means by that creed:

> *"When I was teaching basketball, I urged my players to try their hardest to improve on that very day, to make that practice a masterpiece...It begins by trying to make each day count and knowing you can never make up for a lost day." Whenever a player seemed to be dogging it in practice, Coach would tell him, "Don't think you can make up for it by working twice as hard tomorrow. If you have it within your power to work twice as hard, why aren't*

you doing it now?"

I ask you the same question: If you have it within your power to work harder today then you are, then why aren't you doing it? Time is one thing you can never take for granted. I mentioned it in the previous chapter, but it cannot be overstated.

Every minute that passes is another minute gone.

Baseball has been apart of me ever since my dad threw me that plastic ball and I somehow hit it with my big red plastic bat when I was only one year of age. I once believed as a player that if I still had a baseball jersey on my back then I still had a chance to win. I still believe that. I believe that about anything in life. Every breath that you take means that you still have a chance to make your dreams come to life.

If there is one thing we all can agree on it is that time is our only constant. A second is a second for everybody. We all get 24 hours in a day. We always have and we always will. It is what we do with those seconds that matter and that is why we need to value them to the fullest of our ability. We must focus on the time we have. Whether other people are more fortunate or unfortunate then us, we can never let jealousy or envy creep into our thoughts and actions.

Here's a blog post I wrote called, *Who Should You Really Blame?:*

> During my hour of reading this morning at 5:00am I started getting a fair bit agitated. I was getting agitated at people who just want to play the blame game as to why they aren't healthy or why they aren't rich. I hear comments from

people on a daily basis about how life is too hard or there's no time to be healthy or they don't have enough money to eat healthy...and there's a lot of people who focus on all three.

The fact is, the Laws of Nature, gives us all the same thing. It gives us time and results. If we do a certain thing it will give us just results. If we spend more time exercising it will give us better health, same with eating right.

I'm not saying we all are born on the same platform. Some people are born into wealthy families, just a fact of life. But don't blame people who are born into wealth, it isn't their decision. If you're that jealous about it, blame your family for not building great wealth so you could have been born with lots of money. I mean, at one time, those families were not rich. Somewhere along the line in their lineage someone took a risk and earned that money so his family could live without the worry of money.

And, in all honesty, you're much better off not blaming anybody but yourself. So get off the blame train and take action on your new path. Bums on the street have become millionaires. Single moms with a million kids have become millionaires. People from all areas of life, no matter where they started or where they are currently, have made changes and took risks to live better lives and succeeded.

So why can't that be you? It can...but only if you start focusing on the right stuff. Nature gives everybody the same amount of time in the day so start using it more efficiently and stop blaming everything.

If you aren't living your best life right now, that's okay, you can change that. You must be serious about it, though, and you must be willing to take full responsibility for how you use the time you are given.

Conquer Mastery

Mastery is something very few people pursue and I guess that's not a surprise since most people just walk through life in a zombie-like state. Their minds are just reacting to current stimulus with no real thought process or observation. The great thing is that you can reach mastery in any aspect of your life, it is just going to take a lot of hard work and practice.

In a recent University of Colorado Boulder study they tried to determine how people are able to perform with less effort. We've all seen the athletes who make the hard plays just seem so effortless or the teachers who can just lecture fluently on a subject at the drop of a hat.

In the article, *To perform with less effort, practice beyond perfection, says new CU study*, dated February 9, 2012 it states:

> *Whether you are an athlete, a musician or a stroke patient learning to walk again, practice can make perfect, but more practice may make you more efficient, according to a surprising new University of Colorado Boulder study.*
>
> *The study, led by CU-Boulder Assistant Professor Alaa Ahmed,*

looked at how test subjects learned particular arm-reaching movements using a robotic arm. The results showed that even after a reaching task had been learned and the corresponding decrease in muscle activity had reached a stable state, the overall energy costs to the test subjects continued to decrease. By the end of the task, the net metabolic cost as measured by oxygen consumption and carbon dioxide exhalation had decreased by about 20 percent, she said.

"The message from this study is that in order to perform with less effort, keep on practicing, even after it seems as if the task has been learned," said Ahmed of CU-Boulder's integrative physiology department. "We have shown there is an advantage to continued practice beyond any visible changes in performance."

Now, we have all heard and know the saying, "practice makes perfect", but now I guess we can say, "once you've reached perfect even more practice makes it a lot easier."

Practice The Right Way

There is another factor to practice and getting better every day. When you practice it is crucial you do the right practice. When you take a step back and look at what progress really is I think you can safely come to the conclusion that it is not really how much you practice that matters, but how fast you can fix the errors that are preventing that progression.

In an article from the Time Magazine website, *The Myth of 'Practice Makes Perfect'*, written January 25, 2012 by Annie Murphy Paul, she refers to an article titled *"It's Not How Much; It's How."* The study Paul is referring to was published in the

Journal of Research in Music Education in 2009. Robert Duke, University of Texas-Austin professor and his colleagues "videotaped advanced piano students as they practiced a difficult passage from a Shostakovich concerto, then ranked the participants by the quality of their ultimate performance."

The article goes on to say:

> *The researchers found no relationship between excellence of performance and how many times the students had practiced the piece or how long they spent practicing. Rather, "the most notable differences between the practice sessions of the top-ranked pianists and the remaining participants," Duke and his coauthors wrote, "are related to their handling of errors."*
>
> *The best pianists, they determined, addressed their mistakes immediately. They identified the precise location and source of each error, then rehearsed that part again and again until it was corrected. Only then would the best students proceed to the rest of the piece. "It was not the case that the top-ranked pianists made fewer errors at the beginning of their practice sessions than did the other pianists," Duke notes. "But, when errors occurred, the top-ranked pianists seemed much better able to correct them in ways that precluded their recurrence."*
>
> *Without deliberate practice, even the most talented individuals will reach a plateau and stay there. For most of us, that's just fine. But don't delude yourself that you'll see much improvement unless you're ready to tackle your mistakes as well as your successes.*

Anything we would like to achieve and master we must

approach it properly and with a focus on improving every day by fixing the errors that are stopping us from getting where we want to go. Will that be easy? Not at all. It will be incredibly tough actually - feeling impossible most of the time - but that's just the reality we must accept to move forward aggressively.

There were times when I remember practicing at 5:00am in our domed football stadium because our bus for the airport was leaving at 8:30am. In the fall we would take hundreds of ground balls every day and be insane about our form during fundamentals - our fielding technique warmups. Same with hitting. While we would get a bunch of swings in, we were usually focused on the quality of our swings, not the quantity. We would have a system in place and we would do it.

The hardest part about it was sometimes the end of the tunnel looked blurry and distant. You may be familiar with that feeling. We would begin training in late August when our first game wasn't until mid-February. So on those long, hot September days or those freezing cold January days we spent inside on the football field, it was at times difficult to understand why we had to run a certain play for the thousandth time in the last five months.

It wasn't until game one when it finally dawned on us why all the hours we put in were necessary. For one, it was because that's what was needed to attempt reaching team excellence, but the other reason was because every team we would be playing was doing the same thing. The only question was, "who was working harder?"

This could be true in your life and work. You have to ask yourself, "Have I done everything I can to get myself a promotion if it becomes available?" or "Am I working harder then my competition?" There are hundreds of questions you can ask, but the main question is, "Are you doing everything you possibly can to be your very best?"

The amount of time you spend on your craft could be the scariest factor of all. Since time is such a precious thing, as we don't know how much we have, spending time on getting better at something feels risky. I mean, what if you spend all that time working towards something and then you don't get it or you don't win?

Well, I believe that has to do with a backwards perspective. Every person who has ever reached success in their field or skill will always tell you it was the journey that made it all worthwhile, and if they had to go through all the ups and downs again they would in a heart beat. All those people had moments where it seemed over - their dream was crushed - but they battled and continued to work.

What about the people that never make it though? They dedicate their life to something and then just like that, it's over. It has happened to me with my playing career in baseball. During my junior year I tore my hamstring while playing at the University of Northern Iowa. It proved to be the beginning of the end of my baseball career, which many thought would turn into a very successful professional career. I had already been battling depression at that point but the day I blew up my hamstring was the day I began my collapse mentally. I turned to alcohol even more and my depression catapulted to incredible heights. It was not a proud time in my life, but it was a time I reflect on and I am extremely proud of myself for putting a halt to my negative direction.

In a few months I realized that my negative attitude

wasn't my true path. I had been learning and practicing baseball for 20 years and it was suddenly gone. I continued playing, of course, but the scouts had vanished and nobody really wanted to take a chance on a wounded player - that's how bad my hamstring injury actually was. Plus I kept re-tearing it as I kept playing after the initial rehab didn't fully heal my original injury.

I will tell you the journey was worth every drop of blood, sweat, and tears; there was plenty of all three. I grew as a person and it allowed me to play the highest level of college baseball you can play. I worked hard to get there and because of that journey I learned the effort necessary to achieve great things and the vast amount of time involved to even give yourself the chance to reach your goal.

I used to take hundreds of swings in my backyard almost every night. I would play catch with my dad every night after dinner. I spent hours and hours outside in our driveway throwing a tennis ball against the brick wall of our house. I would play a full imaginary game, make amazing plays - if I do say so myself - and win the World Series almost every time I was out there.

I would read books on baseball and watch instructional DVD's. I remember growing up we owned a VHS called *The Baseball Bunch* and it was hosted by Johnny Bench, the catcher for the Cincinnati Reds. I watched it over and over. The Kool-Aid man himself made appearances and the San Diego Chicken was always there being a hilarious chicken. What wasn't there to love about it? Some of the greatest stars from that era were teaching me how to pitch and field. It was magical. The highlight videos they had were so 80's they would probably be considered cool again; they were bad.

My journey as a baseball player played a huge role molding me into the person I am today. I went through some amazing ups - winning the Junior College World Series - and some severe lows - my career ending hamstring tear. They all taught me something. That's what life is all about. Nothing is ever guaranteed and that's the beauty of it. You can do all the right things and still come up short. It sucks, but it's true.

A lot has to do with how you react to the down moments. If you go and hide in a dark corner you are failing yourself and your potential. If you reflect and learn from it then you are now in the situation to fix the error and move forward. A huge part about getting better every day is recognizing and fixing your errors - immediately, if possible.

In Daniel Coyle's book, *The Talent Code,* he reveals how greatness isn't born. It is grown by how you create your skill by efficiently fixing errors. Coyle talks about the legendary coach John Wooden (who's already been mentioned several times in this book) and how he ran his practices so meticulously. He ran five to fifteen minute drills all while telling players quick phrases to immediately fix whatever mistakes he had just witnessed. Wooden wasn't about long, detailed instruction. He would show how he wanted a skill to be performed, then show how not to perform it, then finish by re-showing the correct form.

Once his short explanations were taught, the players would then get to work and Wooden would target specific errors quickly and accurately with a *'this, not that'* and *'here, not there'* approach. Wooden is quoted as saying, "Don't look for the big, quick improvement. Seek small improvement one day at a time. That's the only way it happens - and when it happens, it lasts."

Your Current Situation

Doing the wrong thing over and over again will slowly ingrain itself to a bad habit, but there is another way to look at it. Your philosophy - what causes you to do what you do - has brought you to your current situation, which means every decision you make can be the difference between your success and your failure. You have to be smart in your philosophy. Now, that might seem like an obvious statement, but in reality it is a statement most people ignore completely.

I mean, what if eating a carrot every day led to perfect vision?

What if reading one hour a day prevented any risk of dementia or Alzheimer's?

What if only thirty minutes of fairly vigorous exercise a day literally vanished all chances of illness and disease?

It would be pretty easy to make the time to do all of those things wouldn't it? If you could prevent mental illness with just one hour of reading a day that nights reality TV show suddenly seems a tad less important, doesn't it?

Here is what I am trying my best to portray for you: Generally what's easy to do is also easy not to do.

It is pretty easy to find some reading time, but it is also pretty easy to put it aside for another day because your favourite movie is on television for the hundredth time. It is easy to get a good exercise session in, but it is also easy to say you're just 'not feeling it today'. That piece of fruit could be staring you right in the face but that chocolate chip cookie in the jar sounds a lot tastier at the current moment.

It is the same for almost everything.

Water or diet pop? "One more set" or "that's good enough for today"? "I'm too tired to get out of bed" or "time to work"?

The list can go on and on and the truth is your decisions will leave lasting impacts. I have gone through a few phases during my life when it was easy for me to say no to working out. Either because it was a long day of work or because something on my body was nagging me from a past injury. I would find a little time in the day when a workout would do me wonders but I would decide that I really needed the rest instead. So instead of 4-5 workouts a week I'd get anywhere from 1-3, and they weren't anything to write home about.

After a while I was getting weaker and skinnier (I wasn't going for weight loss). It was from just a few errors in judgment that I gradually started paying the price. I did not feel as good as I used too, it was horrible, but it was easy to continue playing the victim and continue telling myself that, "I am working long days" and "need to take a break anytime I can get it."

The decisions we make between ultimate health and a gradual destruction stem from simple, daily decisions. You have to be wise and realize what role your current decisions are playing on your future. I remember Jim Rohn once saying, "What if somebody got it mixed up and thought it was a Hershey bar a day, keeps the doctor away? You gotta be smarter in your philosophy." A few decisions in judgment repeated everyday can be the difference between a happy and healthy future or a disastrous constant battle with sickness.

Our Mortality

Our own mortality and the acceptance of it is the surest form of reality. It will help you forget all the meaningless stuff that happens during a day or negative thoughts that prevent you from pursuing something; whether you fear failure or not.

Dreams mean nothing without action. Love means nothing without compassion. Effort means nothing without purpose. Hope means nothing without belief.

Death scares people. When a person close to us dies we feel great sadness and it causes us to reflect on our lives because the death of that person tells us something very real; it is going to happen to us one day too.

Some people react with an initial bit of inspiration to change something about their life they don't like, but that wears off somewhat quickly once 'real' life gets back into full force. There are some people who feel the sadness and just move on with what they are doing without much refection at all. Then there are those few who actually do start making a change that they feel is necessary to create a more fulfilling life for themselves. That's what makes life so unique. Everybody has different reactions to the same thing. It is fascinating to me.

When my Grandpa Grant died it hit me pretty hard. There were random days three years after his death when I would just break down crying, thinking about the impact he left on our family and so many other people. I was recently back home and visited his old business which he started after he retired from teaching at 65. His picture is still proudly hung in the office with a great caption reflecting on what he left behind.

When he passed I did a lot of reflecting and thinking. I was 23 years old and at a turning point of my life. I just finished and graduated from the University of Northern Iowa and was now back at home in Thunder Bay, Ontario, Canada. His funeral is seared in my mind. I cried uncontrollably during the service, especially when my Grandpa Schmidt (who performed the sermon) talked about what I had written about my Grandpa Grant in my player profile. That player profile was featured in the game program one weekend at Northern Iowa. When asked who my greatest influence was I said, "My grandpa because he never stopped working and always found time to be there, for not only myself, but his whole family."

I thought I had composed myself once the funeral had ended and I reluctantly left the pew to walk outside, but when we got outside the church there was a full bagpipe band standing on the front lawn of City Hall playing a tribute to my grandpa. It was surreal. I remember people coming up to me and shaking my hand. They were telling me nice things about my Grandpa Grant and I did everything I could to keep a strong face, but it was impossible. I could not speak and tried to hide my tears behind my sunglasses.

It was at that moment with the amazing music filling the air that I realized how much my grandpa made an impact in the community. Members of Parliament were there. The mayor of Thunder Bay and former mayors were there. It amazed me, and I knew that I wanted to make an impact like he did. He is a big reason why I write the type of material I do and strongly believe in my message, because I want to make a difference, just like he did. I have a picture of him in my bedroom and every once in awhile I'll look at him and reflect on what I am doing or what I should be doing.

To say it was an instant change in my life's course would be wrong, however. It took time to change and be confident in both my perspectives and direction. It took years to finally feel like I was making progress in my mission. I don't think I will ever be satisfied with where I am going or what I am doing. I hope I never am. I don't think Grandpa Grant was. He always tried to make things better and make a difference. That's what I want to do.

If during your reflections you feel the need to make a change, then make it. Just understand it could take years before you feel like you are actually making the right moves and going in the right direction for yourself.

If you're worried about losing friends or making people angry then let me share with you a quick story to ease your mind.

At a coffee shop one day I overheard a conversation a group of older gentlemen were having. They were probably in their 80's and they were talking about death. One man said, "Do you remember Eddie? Good lord, he was a mean ole' bugger. Hated everything and everybody. Nobody liked him, but at his funeral the church was overflowing with people. Isn't it funny how everybody likes you after you're dead?"

I couldn't help but chuckle a bit at what the man just said and the truth of his statement. All of our faults will be told as funny stories after we are gone. So if you need comfort, our actions are almost always remembered that way; a funny story. Everybody is going to love you no matter what. Awesome, right?

We Live To Serve

You cannot just focus on getting yourself better every day. You have to help other people as well. I spent some time living in Nanaimo, British Columbia, Canada and from my place to downtown was a beautiful walk along the harbour. During the brisk winter in late January it's not too busy but there are still plenty of people walking and enjoy the ocean. One thing I noticed was how so many people walk with their head down, refusing to make eye contact or say good morning in return of my initiating this pleasantry.

I'm not saying I would say hello to everybody - sometimes I was lost in thought or looking off somewhere. If for some reason I was paying full attention and I heard a good morning towards me I would always reply. I do my best to at least have a smile on my face when people look my way.

People just look so scared and depressed these days. Some of these very people could learn a quick lesson on enjoying the moment by looking down at their dogs. Those guys are smiling and friendly, just happy to be out and about going for a nice walk. I think people need to start appreciating a pleasant walk more often.

You never know, maybe someone is having a really bad day and your smile may somehow lift his or her spirits a little. That in a way is helping them get a little better.

You Can't Go Half Polite

We all ask people when we see them, "How are you doing?"

We all ask it, but we don't all listen to the reply. This is sometimes tough to do. We could be in a hurry and bump into somebody in a store or about to head out the door and we get a call from a friend. We ask them how they are but our minds are still focused on where we have to go or how late we might be. I know I can tell when someone is not paying attention to me speak and I am sure they can tell if my mind is elsewhere. It doesn't feel good when you know the person you are talking too doesn't care enough to really listen, especially if they were the ones who asked the question.

Yes, it is polite to ask how people are feeling, but it is not polite to then not listen. You can't only be half polite. You have to be 'full' polite. It is challenging sometimes but it is necessary to making people feel good to be being a person with great character. Not listening turns a courteous and polite moment into a pointless one, and pointless is the vain of our existence right now. So many things we do are pointless. Surfing mindlessly on the internet, watching stupid television shows, gossiping about a friend behind their back, texting while driving, etc. Sure it might be okay to be pointless when you are alone, but it should never be pointless if you are with or talking to another person. Your time is not more valuable than theirs, even if you are 'worth' more monetarily. Be present with people.

To continue my rant - it is far from over - never ask a question because you know that person will reply with the same question so you can spew on them how crappy and hard your life is. If you want to make sure it is hard to find people to complain too then I would recommend you always divulge all the negativity about your life. Nothing will get people ignoring you like a constant shower of unimportant drama and controlled negativity.

Don't be a glossy eyed arrogant prick when listening and having a conversation with people, especially - and underline especially - if it is with your significant other. Disrespecting your wife, husband, boyfriend, girlfriend is the epitome of arrogance. Unfortunately, there are times when it will happen even if you don't mean it too, but if you do it on purpose then you need to start looking inside and figuring out what kind of person you really are.

Be Original and Make A Difference In People's Lives

After you have listened and feel you have valuable advice for that person then give it. Whether they take the advice or not is their call. I remember there was a time when I felt bad if people did not take my advice. For some reason I thought I had failed them. I have come to learn no matter how good or bad your advice is, it is up to the person receiving it to put it into action.

Part of the reason I think so many people are unhappy is because they do not feel heard. They have people all day asking the same question and then giving them the same mundane response. That's sad. At least take the time develop an original answer that can help that person in someway, whether it be encouragement or extra excitement to get them even more thrilled about what they are doing. That feels good and part of helping people get better every single day is making them feel good about themselves.

Your Significant Other Is The Most Important Person So Treat Them That Way

If you're in a relationship, show how much you love and care for the other person. Take time to tell her/him how you feel or how good she/he looks. Get her some flowers. Sacrifice through watching his favourite sport for a while even if you would rather stab yourself in the eye with a fork. A lot of relationships do not spend time actually trying to have the best relationship they can. They get comfortable over time, going through the motions, which eventually turns it into a mediocre relationship. Why would you want that?

Motivational speaker and author Zig Ziglar once said, "Many marriages would be better if the husband and the wife clearly understood that they are on the same side." Work daily at creating a unique and special relationship with the love of your life. Buying chocolates on Valentine's Day and taking her out for dinner is something that should be happening throughout the year. If it only happens once a year I beg you to analyze why that is. Be spontaneous and try new things together. There is no rule book out there that says dinner and a movie should make up the majority of your date nights.

Make Your Day Perfect By Making Another Person's Day Perfect

Coach John Wooden said, "You have not lived a perfect day until you've done something for somebody who cannot repay you." I think that pretty much in one sentence summarizes what this part of the chapter is about.

I have already told you that I am selfish about my books and do not just lend them. If I find a book that I feel will help somebody I know, I will tell them about it or I will buy it for them. In the past I have done plenty of secret book buys where someone will just happen to find a book on their desk or even in their mailbox.

These days with iTunes it is easy to send someone a good song or even an audiobook. You can do it all through email, it is amazing. It is simple and could make a humongous difference in someone's day. I have friends and family email me for fitness or life advice all the time. Every once in a while I like to email them a full fitness program or an interview I did. It is a good feeling to be able to give this to them.

Have you ever been in a coffee drive-thru and got to the payment window only to be informed the person in front of you paid for your coffee? It is a pretty cool feeling and makes you want to pay for the persons coffee behind you - which you should do, by the way.

Now would be a great time to reflect and think when the last time you have surprised somebody with a special gift or some kind words. Why has it been so long? It could be done with a quick call to tell them how important they are to you or how much their advice has helped you. It could be a short letter that shows up in their mailbox one day. We have to be careful not to get caught up in our own lives and forget about the people around us. If your life feels so monotonous and boring that you do not have the energy to help another person, then it is time you get your life figured out and make immediate changes.

Our lives should be about helping people out. That is why I coach and why I am writing this book. To help. It would be pointless for me to spend the hours upon hours it has taken me to put my thoughts into words if I did not feel in my heart that it would help somebody.

Take the time to get better every day and stop wishing life could be easier. Take control of your body and your life. Never miss an opportunity to help someone out. Your life is your journey. Every day is a page in your book. Make sure you make the most out of each page so at the end of your life, your book leaves a legacy like no other.

CHAPTER SEVEN

PERSONAL GREATNESS

"No great man ever complains of want of opportunity." Ralph Waldo Emerson

"The price of greatness is responsibility." Winston Churchill

"I will show no mercy-nor have any belief whatsoever in how others judge me...for my greatness will silence them all." - Warrior

When it comes to Warrior (former WWE professional wrestler and his real name legally, by the way), there are no in between feelings whether people love or hate him. It is one of the two, and that is it. I personally love Warrior, and the quote I added before this first paragraph fires me up. This chapter is the last step until your first move forward. I have told you my story and I have taught you the strategies I used to defeat my severe depression and anxiety, and continue to use today to keep me on the winning side. The depression and anxiety may never fully leave me - it certainly can, however - but the habits I built have created the walls that will block any attacks that may occur.

If you have been struggling with any aspect of your life, what I have written will help you if you put them into action. In reality, most people are afraid of making a move or taking a risk. It is scary and uncomfortable - two things we naturally hate. When you are trying to change your life it takes a unique level of hard work and discipline. It is an intensely daunting and formidable task. When it comes to your life you are the sole leader of the new path you are creating. Sure, people can and will influence progress. Ultimately it is you that will be making the choices and doing the real work.

The work and discipline, however, is the easy part. The hard part is the emotional toll that it will have on you. You are now on the path towards powerful change and once you start making progress people will become jealous. They will not understand why you are doing what you are doing, so they may start poking fun at you or telling you how wrong you are. You will get the big promotion, earn a huge income, or reach top health and they will sit there and call you 'lucky.'

They will never understand the blood, sweat, and tears that you mentality and physically brought to the table to achieve what you did. They will never understand the bumps and the bruises you took to get where you wanted to go. They will never comprehend how the failures made you stronger and how you crawled through the mud and dirt to get the opportunity to be so close to your dream you could touch it. These are the people who have always been too scared to try. The important thing to remember is it doesn't matter how it looks to other people. It only matters how it looks to you.

Too Many, Too Scared

Most people, as I have mentioned numerous times already, aren't willing to take the bumps, accept failure, and move forward. When I was working through my personal issues, change did not happen immediately after I made the decision to take the first steps. It took years. It took sitting through dinners where my anxiety was so high I would have to cut pieces of meat the width of a nail and the length smaller than a dime to be able to force it down. I would have people bombarding me with questions concerning if I liked the food or if everything was all right. I sat there and did the best I could. It was horrible and embarrassing, but it was a part of my process. I put myself in situations I was having major difficulties with and did what I could when I was in them. Even today, anxiety pounds on my door and I hate to say that sometimes it wins, but it does. It is rare that it will, but it can.

During my process of healing, especially at the beginning, I had to make lifestyle decisions I felt necessary to aid my growth. It lost some 'friends'. Creating a simple lifestyle was what I needed, so I decided to let certain things go. I was judged by the people who did not understand why I could not party with them or even hang out with them anymore. These people will dislike your changes the most, but that is okay. You are moving forward and people get sensitive when they are not seen as important anymore. They will judge you, talk behind your back, and flat out lie to your face with a weak grin when they tell you how happy they are for you. They can be family members or people who have worn masks of friendship your whole life.

They will tell you that your life is fine just the way it is. They will make off-handed remarks towards your mission to poke fun at you. They will question why you need to eat so healthy or why you don't get smashed with them anymore.

They will be unhappy that instead of hanging out to gossip, you are working your ass off trying to attain your personal greatness. They will stay at their same level of existence while you are climbing, and the distance you create will turn into a decision you will have to make: Do you go back or do you say goodbye and keep moving forward? Making it to this point of the book means that you want to live, not just be alive. Forward you go.

Truth, Death, and Just Doing The Best You Can

There is no denying that we are all going to be dead one day. I don't want to put a damper on anything but it is true. It is the cycle of life and there is no way around it. That is why it is crucial to never let outside influences affect your progress. The only person who should be allowed to have any say would be your husband or wife because you chose to marry them which means everything is now a team decision. Everybody else, however, can have advice or opinions, but that should never hold you back for any reason. Even if it feels like a good decision right now, whether to save a relationship or just make the other person happy at the moment, it is going to hurt you in the long run.

I tell all my clients: *Never stop challenging yourself to achieve your own personal greatness. That is the only form of greatness that truly matters.*

One of the challenges in continuing to strive towards that greatness is the consistent belief you have in yourself. It took me a long time to believe that I could do what I wanted. It happens to everybody and I think that is part of what makes life so great. We all have our doubts and insecurities. We all have our flaws too. I have my fair share of insecurities that challenge me on a daily basis. I used to let them crush me and grind me into a dust of lost hope. It used to be scary to write my thoughts down and then share them with people. I used to get upset if I received an email that disagreed with my opinions. I used to think I was too young to be a leader of anything. Some of those thoughts will still pass through my mind when I am writing a piece for an article or a project.

The difference today is I let the thought pass through and do not let it consume my mind. I accept the thought, chuckle a little bit, and then continue writing. That reaction did not happen overnight either. It took years of hard work and discipline to push past those thoughts.

Albert Einstein said, "We have to do the best we can. This is our sacred human responsibility." You must take full responsibility over your life. You are who you currently are because of the past decisions you have made. That is a fact. Until you accept that you will never be able to reach your best life. Every decision you make today can change and shape your future.

You Can Live More Then One Act

There will forever be ups and downs during our life. Some of the greatest creators and people of all time have had to overcome adversity most people think would be impossible to overcome.

Winston Churchill is a man you can honestly say never quit. Churchill was at first recognized as a rising star in his early decades in politics. In the 1930's, however, he was not even in office and could not get in. He then became infamous for his leadership during World War II but in 1945 he lost his office by a landslide victory to the opposition. That would usually crush even the strongest of politicians, but Churchill never gave up and in 1951 was elected back into office as the Prime Minister.

Frank Sinatra - ol' blue eyes, himself - once retired because of poor success. A couple years later he made a comeback and resurrected his career. I am a big Sinatra fan. How can you not love, *My Way*?

I call it your 'Second Act'. Churchill you could say had more like three acts. The point is, when things are not going your way or if you do get knocked down it is imperative that you get back up. There are no second chances at this life so you have to make your whole time here count.

My life in baseball started when I was extremely young. My parents gave me one of those plastic red bats when I was one year old and I nearly broke a window the first time I ever held that thing. "No hitting in the house" was the rule from an early age. My dad taught me everything I knew when it came to baseball. When I went away to play college baseball at Parkland Community College in Champaign, Illinois my career began to surge. My sophomore year we won the Junior College World Series, I was named World Series M.V.P., and 1st-Team All-American, along with a bunch of other awards. I had a lot of scouts and universities looking at me and I felt great about my future in baseball.

I received a scholarship my junior year to the University of Northern Iowa and started the season on fire. Then, three weeks in I tore my hamstring in crippling fashion and all the Major League scouts who were interested had suddenly disappeared. I was devastated. I will never forget being pulled the last game of that year in the Conference Tournament because I was struggling so bad. I came back playing too early that season and I was never the same. I actually kept tearing my hamstring as I continued to play.

My senior year was a success in many ways. I was second on the team in batting average, hitting .342, and I lead the team in home runs, doubles, and runs batted in. My playing career was finished, though. I got a review done by a hamstring specialist and was told that my hamstring was in such bad shape that I should never play high-level baseball ever again or I would not be able to walk by the time I was thirty.

I listened and started my career in the fitness industry. Every spring that rolled around after was like a punch to my gut. I felt empty and deep down knew why, but I never did anything about it. My head was tied up in too many thoughts about career, relationships, and the actual ability to walk later on in life. Then something hit me. That punch to my gut every spring just kept getting heavier and harder and I knew I had to retire from baseball on my own terms.

So in true Rocky Balboa fashion I started training and going to some tryouts. I ended up finding a gig in Sherwood Park, Alberta, Canada for the summer. I ended up winning the league M.V.P. award and received some great European pro offers and an offer in the Atlantic League. But I stuck to my promise and retired officially from playing after that year. I felt at peace about the whole thing. I restarted a new fitness business in Edmonton, Alberta, Canada and ran that for a few years.

In January of 2011 I was inducted in Parkland Colleges Athletic Hall of Fame. It is one of the greatest honours of my life and I love the fact that I'm 'immortal' if only in a small way. Around that time of the induction ceremonies and reminiscing about the old days of college baseball something started to happen again. The punching came back. It is probably best to describe this new round of mythical beatings more like swift kicks to the gut. When that happens I know it is because I should be doing something else in my life. I knew what that was and as an added bonus, my wife was all for it. It was awesome.

It was not playing that I wanted to do. It was coaching. It was my 'second act' in baseball. Going back was great and inspired me to continue doing fitness coaching and write even more. I enjoyed it every single day and I was not getting the crap beat out of me from my subconscious Bruce Lee. I now write, coach people to their best health, and still help coach baseball.

Everybody can have a 'second act'. Your 'second act' can be anything you want it to be. You can move on from the past and create a grand new future for yourself or you can go back to the thing you used to love most and reinvent yourself to conquer that life once again

Potential Means Nothing

"What we are to be really, we are now potentially", writes Orison Swett Marden in his 1896 masterpiece, *Pushing To The Front*. Typically, we all have heroes or mentors in our field of work that we look up to and learn from. In the baseball world, a man I respect greatly is Texas Longhorns baseball coach Augie Garrido. Augie is the winningest coach in NCAA Division I history. One of my favourite stories about potential comes from one of Augie's experiences when he first got hired by the Longhorns after becoming known as the best college baseball coach out there due to his epic success coaching Cal State Fullerton.

In Augie's book, *Life Is Yours to Win,* he tells the story:

> *When the 'Horns were tanking and I was struggling during my first year as their coach, Darrell Royal, the Longhorns' retired football coach and athletic director, stopped by during practice. A legend on campus and across the country, Coach Royal never had a losing season in twenty years of coaching at UT, where the football stadium rightfully bears his name.*
>
> *"What sort of team will you have this year, Coach?" he asked.*
>
> *I had no idea, so I hemmed and hawed and finally mumbled something about having some great athletes with a lot of potential.*
>
> *Royal's face reddened. He looked down at his boots, then turned his laser gaze on me. "You know, boy, that poh-tential you're talkin' 'bout right there will get your ass fired around here."*
> *I should have chosen my words more carefully. This was, after all, the same coach famous for saying, "Potential means you ain't done nothin' yet."*
>
> *No wonder college coaches tend to flinch when they hear a scout, a*

parent, or a high school coach tout someone as having "great potential." Too often, it means that they're pushing someone who is gifted but not engaged, a prospect but not a player.

After doing some of my own research on Coach Royal I found he was also famous among his players for saying, "Never take a lazy step." I think that is such a great quote. As Garrido stated at the end of the story above, most people who are said to have "great potential" are usually prospects not players. To create your own personal greatness you must be a player.

You would not want to be known as the person with so much promise and talent would you? I hope not. I think you would rather be known as the person who is what they are. Everybody has potential; we just need to make sure that potential turns into results.

The Legacy Reflection

Life is crazy. Your temporary moment in time – if you can believe 'time' is real – that can leave a ripple effect on multiple generations. I used to preach legacy, and I still actually do, but just differently. I was all about legacy this and legacy that. If you were not working hard to leave a legacy for this world than you were not living right. One night - while doing nothing in the form of reflection or meditation - an idea flashed in my mind.

Telling people they need to leave a legacy is irrelevant. Why? Because everybody leaves a legacy, regardless of what they do in their moment on earth.

When I realized this, at first I felt a little stupid, but I also felt grateful, because now I can speak differently about legacy. I can teach it better. I can, hopefully, make better connections with people now that I understand this.

Think about this for a moment. If we give a person bad information and it 'sticks' with them, we have now set off the potential for decades long use of that information. That person could tell their young absorbent child that incorrect information. It will become truth to that young person and it will stay with them, and who knows how many kids they tell about what "their mommy told them." I remember hearing from someone when I was younger that snowmobiles were deathtraps. Every winter there would be one or two stories about deaths caused by snowmobiles. I believed if you road on a snowmobile there was a high risk of going mach speed into trees or poles. Silly, isn't it? But, I have never to this day been on a snowmobile. Even right now thinking about it gives me a nervous energy asking, "why would you ever get on one of those things?"

That person who I heard it from might have had a bad experience with them or knew someone who did. Their information left a legacy of snowmobile hating for me. It is funny, but you have more chance of getting killed by eating a steak then you do by driving a snowmobile. Nobody ever told me steaks were deathtraps.

That is a minor example, of course, but I hope it gives some perspective on what I am saying. I talked to an elderly gentleman the other day about upbringing. He told me he still hears his father - who has been dead for decades - telling him that 'he can't do that' when he is making decisions. This man is over 70 years old and his father is still telling him he will fail. Interesting. Why is society being twisted into this negative ravel of thinking? Because we have stopped thinking. We mainly just accept. Thinking about meaningful stuff is challenging and grips your stomach, wrenching it until it cannot be twisted anymore.

The thought that life is temporary scares that crap out of people. So to distract themselves from that thought, they go back to their thoughtless book or reality TV show. The less we have to think, the better off we are. That seems to be a motto for most of North America, anyways. I cannot really comment on other regions because I have no personal experience with them. While speaking on this for a second, let me expand on leaving a legacy. The snowmobile example was word related. I was told something and it 'stuck' with me. Another facet we need to understand is how our actions leave legacies too. If your young son sees you push your wife what message are you sending? If he sees you drinking and then getting in a car, what does he think is okay behaviour? If he sees you watching crappy TV then why would he want to read a classic Steinbeck novel?

Of course not always will your actions leave an instant 'mark' on another person, but you need to understand that it could. I call it: honest positivity. I add 'honest' because there lies a line that you can cross where it becomes total bullshit positivity. Like when you tell people they can do anything they want. No you can't. A seven-foot man cannot be an astronaut. Laws have continually been created over the years designed to prevent people from doing certain things. You can do them, of course, but it will result in spending sometime in a cold room with metal poles preventing you from going anywhere. If you are questioning stone cold facts, then you are delusional. If you are questioning ideas, then you are being progressive. The impact of decisions made by Presidents decades ago still linger in todays economy and government. Decisions of today greatly affect occurrences of tomorrow. So now is not the time to be lazy with your thoughts and actions.

Honest positivity is saying something like, "Snowmobiles have caused a very small percentage of people to die, but if you're safe and take serious control over it you can have a lot of fun and enjoy riding around on snow." It is showing that it is not okay to risk lives by getting in a driver's seat drunk. Did you read the word *showing* there, not just *telling* - big difference. Holding a door open for someone has the possibility to unlock a mood change in that can have a ripple effect on the people they come in contact with the rest of the day.

Be kind, be helpful, be loving, be truthful, be positive. Leave a legacy that will help people and could help the world. We are all in this together, aren't we?

Leave Your Mark

You can make huge impacts on the world. All it takes is one moment, one song, one poem, one article, one action. What you do in your life leaves a 'mark' and the bigger your 'mark', the more impact you have on the world and the future of it. Typically our biggest moments happen after much preparation and focus.

Some of our greatest heroes that have left a lasting impact are known for one or two big moments. They were not making earth-shattering decisions every day, but it took years of research and forming an opinion to know what they were to do when their action was needed. They created their own greatness by doing the necessary work and having a purpose.

John Fitzgerald Kennedy's (JFK) life ended before it should have when he was assassinated November 22, 1963 in Dallas, Texas. JFK certainly did leave his mark, though. He was always ill growing up and had a major back issue that sometimes totally crippled him. As a Lieutenant in the Navy, his PT-109 was rammed by a Japanese destroyer. There were 12 other men on the command vessel and Kennedy was thrown hard to the deck. Kennedy ordered everyone to abandon ship. When he was able to take a toll on everybody who had gathered at the only part of the boat still afloat there were 10. Two had died in the attack. That is not the end of this story, however. As the sun started coming up, the piece of the boat they were all floating on began to sink and they were forced to abandon. They found a floating eight-foot plank nearby where nine of the crew could hang on to and would also help the members who could not swim. One crewmember was grossly burned during the attack and unable to do much. Kennedy decided he would take him to shore. The others swam holding on to the plank while Kennedy - holding a loose strap of the burned crew members life jacket in his mouth - swam and dragged him for four hours. Once there, Kennedy collapsed and eventually threw up from taking in so much seawater. They were eventually rescued and Kennedy was deemed a hero for his actions.

Come To Grips With Your Own Mortality

This book has been about truth - as far as I see it anyways. Whether you agree with it is up to you. There are times even today when I hesitate when it comes to writing books or letting my opinions be known on certain subject matters. Sometimes it is because it did not seem worth it to share. Other times it is fear based on what people will think.

I am destined for great things in this life - I believe that. I have always been a person who reflects deeply on life. It is one of the reasons why I loved the bus rides traveling around the United States and Canada playing and coaching baseball. I was able to just sit and stare out the window, observing the land and reflecting on anything I chose.

I have always carried with me a great amount of interest in legacy and what greatness really is - and why we consider anything great or not great for that matter. The conclusion that I have come to terms with, when dealing with life and why things are so important to us or why legacy is so necessary, is because of the simple fact that we are all going to die one day.

I find a lot of people do not like thinking about this and are even scared of just the thought, and I was like that too. There is an amazing freedom that presents itself when you understand and come to grips that it will, in fact, happen one day.

Have you ever wondered why beautiful is beautiful? Have you ever asked yourself why certain things are so important to you? Have you ever considered that the fear we try to avoid is because we actually fear the one greatest truth? Why is winning so important? Why is becoming rich so desired by so many people? Why do we cling to relationships that are not necessary? Why do we search for our true love and want it to happen now? Why are we so unhappy in jobs we do not want to do?

The questions, of course, can go on and on. The answer to all of those questions, I believe, is because we know - whether consciously or subconsciously - that we are going to die one day and we need good things to happen to us now because we do not have forever.

If we could live forever then working a job we did not like for thirty years is not that big of a deal because we have an eternity to go. Why would we search for true love if we had forever for it to fall into our laps? Winning championships wouldn't be that big of a deal. All of this health and fitness stuff would be null and void. Nothing would matter if we lived forever. There would be no urgency to do anything and whatever we accomplished would be pretty much meaningless.

To enjoy all the great things and feel that we have the freedom to do something that makes a difference, we must not fear death. It is inevitable. Being scared of certain things will still happen. That is only natural. That is how we are wired as human beings, but with the freedom to understand that we don't really have to be scared. We can move past it and forward on our journey.

Personally, writing this book was scary as hell. I had never really put all my opinions together before. I was fearful about what people would think. Is it just a waste of time? Will this actually help people? What if they think it's too long or too short? What if they don't like the title? What if they don't like the concept? What if, what if, what if?

The great thing about 'what if's?' is they are all self-created and not real. If they do become real, then it means you have finished what you were scared to do. There is power in that. Think about it, if I let the 'what if's?' beat me, then this book would not be in your hands right now.

I beat the fear and now have something to send out to the world to be judged. I can be proud of that. If you want to make a difference I urge you to get started and complete something meaningful for yourself and the world.

Beautiful is beautiful because we have only so much time to enjoy it. We are sometimes so amazed by something it can 'take our breath away.' We feel that because there will be a time when that vision will never be seen again. Death is something we need to accept, so we can enjoy the magic and beauty life has to offer and stop hiding behind our fears that keep us in the shadows.

CHAPTER EIGHT

THE NEW PRESENT

Everything is black. I have just woken up. I hear nothing. My legs feel a heavy pressure on top to them and I can't force them to move. I open my eyes and stare momentarily at the dark ceiling, which is only dark because it is still pitch black outside. I carefully tilt my head up to glance down at my immovable legs and see my dog Lily draped across them.

I drop my head back down allowing me to gaze up towards the ceiling once again. I'm tired. I know once I get into standing position the sleepiness will begin to fade. I attempt rolling over on my right side but the weight of Lily prevents even a minimal movement, so I continue to just lay still, trying not to fall back asleep. It is 4:15am, and it is time to read and write. I see if bending my knee will somehow cause Lily to roll down my leg or at least be annoyed enough to shuffle into a new sleep position. It did not work. She is still passed out and I am starting to wonder if the battle to relieve my legs from her weight is worth it. A professional, I decide, would get out and get to work. So the decision is now based on whether I will be an amateur today or a professional. To be a professional means doing your work no matter what. An amateur does his work when he has time, or feels like it. Being a professional is a lot harder, and it is a lot more rewarding. The problem is sometimes sacrifices need to be made so you can ensure you get your work done. In this case, Lily's comfort.

During my sudden moment of inspiration contemplating my desire to be a professional writer, I give a forceful thrust pulling both my knees up causing my poor puppy to hurl sideways onto her ribs and squint at me with both confusion and disgust in her sleepy almond shaped eyes. I give a quiet, borderline unemotional, "I'm sorry Lily", and watch as she ignores my apology and collapses her basenji head back onto the comforter.

My first step out of bed feels good, my second step shocks me with reminders of an old nagging hamstring injury. By step 12 the ache starts to dissipate - roughly about the time I reach the coffee pot. Once I dig out two scoops of single origin coffee from my favourite local coffee shop, Cafe Fantastico, I press the brew button and head towards the computer on this particular Sunday morning. I check my email and head towards a couple news sites to see if anything worth thinking about is happening around the world. Usually there is not. Not to say I do not care about the problems and issues happening in the world, but today it is not something I am ready to do anything about so I am not going to allow it to enter my 'fear' bubble and wreck the way I live my life.

I load up my blogs dashboard and reflect on a probable blog post. My reflections veer towards the fact that we do not realize how fragile our lives are. Sure, we have been around for thousands of years, but at virtually any moment something could happen to wipe a percentage of us off the planet. I decide that I like the thought but will it cause a fear based reaction?

My coffee is ready and I pour myself a full cup and carry it back to my desk. I stare at the screen and momentarily picture our planet floating about in space with a gazillion stars and millions of planets and billions of asteroids flying around and I wonder why we are so egotistical and so worried. In the end will any of it matter? When there is no Earth, what was it all for? Why is money so important to people or make people feel so elite? Of course, I'm not saying money is bad, it has its benefits. It gives you the ability to enjoy stability with certain aspects of life. Some amazingly fun aspects too. Whether you have money or not, more than likely you are going to be the same person. With money you are just amplified. If you are an asshole, then you are an asshole with money and that is probably the how you got it. At least, that is what a lot of people will think. If you are an asshole and poor, you are just an asshole and that is probably why you are poor. Doesn't this all sound silly? This is 99% of people's view on money and people. Our minds have been corrupted and coerced into believing silly stuff that shouldn't matter in OUR lives. Who cares if someone has money? Who cares if the asshole is poor? An asshole is an asshole. That is reality and that is the way we should view life, because in the end we were given an opportunity to help mankind in some way. Whether we did or not was up to us. If you didn't, then you didn't. If you did, then you did. Nobody cares about why you did or why you didn't, they just care about the results you helped produce.

Sorry, sometimes I ramble. Of course, the above thoughts are something that just could be in my next book and maybe - just maybe - it could be called, *The War on Self 2 - The Philosophical Edition*. You never know.

After I write down some thoughts I pick up the book I'm reading, *On Writing*, by Stephen King. It is part memoir, part how-to write stories well. Unfortunately for you this book was written before I have finished reading it. An hour passes and it is time for some more writing. Rewriting and editing of one of my short stories to be exact. The story is called, *Standing In The Shade*, and the plan is to release it on my blog.

It is now nearing 6:30am. At this point I will either be going for cup of coffee number two or start thinking about eating something. Every morning is not the same. I always have different writing and projects going on. Today I am not going to a doctor, taking any medication, or telling my problems to a soft spoken dude with glasses. I am doing my own thing, walking my own path. If it works then awesome. If it doesn't I will keep working and building new things and new ideas. I will speak my mind and help whomever I can help. The amazing news is this is only the start. My wonder and excitement for this life and this world is not going to stop until I am dead, and I am not planning on that being anytime soon.

Be wondrous, create awesome things, and be a person who loves this grand life and all the possibilities that can come with it. But most importantly, enjoy this ride.

ACKNOWLEDGEMENTS

To my wife, Karlee. You have been my rock throughout this whole process. This book could not have been written without your constant love, support, and input. My dear, you dealt with me when I needed to vent or chat about this book and when I would stare blankly into the distance with thoughts and frustrations consuming me. Thank you beautiful, I love you with all my heart! I can't thank my parents, Alex and Debbie, enough for the upbringing I had. As kids we were given everything we needed and were cheered and supported during all the ups and downs, from our competitive sports competitions to our crazy life decisions. I love you.

To my brother, Mark, and my sister, Ashley. I'm lucky to have a brother and a sister like you two. Mark, with all my outlandish thoughts and ideas, never once did you question any of them. You gave me the confidence to pursue any dream or goal I've ever had. Ashley, you are an amazing sister and the talks we've had through all of our tough times helped me push through. I hope that I've helped you the same.

To my Grandma and Grandpa Schmidt. I love you both so much. You have been my inspiration throughout this writing process. I hope you like it. Your advice and love mean the world to me.

To my Grandma and Grandpa Grant. I love you and miss you both. Thank you for believing in me. I wish you were still here to read this.

To my best friend in the whole wide world, Justin Griffith. We met one sunny day inside a small gym when we became workmates. We didn't talk much to each other for two months until you invited me to an NHL game. Since then your friendship has meant everything. Even though your really weird nuances can draw great confusion from me, you are my favourite dude ever, and I love you sir. Not as much as you love Ryan Gosling, however. And to Mary Griffith, thanks for letting me sleep on your couch when I needed to, thanks for cooking me dinner when I was around, and thanks for yelling at me when I needed a yelling.

I've had many great coaches over the years. My dad, who taught me everything I knew about baseball growing up. He sacrificed every night after dinner taking me out into the backyard or the street to play catch, and coaching me until I went to college. To all my baseball coaches throughout the years, mainly Bruce Barber, Rod Lovett, Dave Seifert, and Rick Heller. Your leadership and instruction shaped me into the ball player I was and gave me the courage to dive into the coaching field myself. Bo Bundrick, even during my short time in Virginia you left a lasting impact on me. Garnet Hansen, thank you for giving me a shot as a college head coach. I'm eternally grateful to you for making one of my dreams come true.

To all the players I've played with and coaches I've played for, thank you for the good times, the rough times, the laughs, and the cries. Hanging out and listening to all the jokes and stories is what I miss the most. You all made my experience in baseball a unique and memorable one. I still smile often thinking back on all the amazing memories.

ABOUT THE AUTHOR

Daniel CJ Grant is a writer, fitness professional, baseball coach, and dreamer. He has an Associates Degree in Science from Parkland Community College and a Bachelor of Arts in Physical Education from the University of Northern Iowa. He has had articles featured in *Inside Fitness Magazine* and *Fine Lifestyles Magazine*. This is his first book.

To contact Dan, please visit his website at
www.danielcjgrant.com

JOIN THE DEPRESSED I AM PROJECT TODAY!

When you join my exclusive newsletter (which is totally free), you get my eBook, *The Positive Side Of Depression,* which also includes two popular articles, *3 Ways To Conquer Your War On Self* and *My Top 3 Tips To Make The Shift,* and three of my short stories.

Sign Up Today by going to my blog at:

www.positivedepression.net

Made in the USA
Monee, IL
04 November 2026

67379800R00085